I0002818

XML & XSL
Fast Start
2nd Edition

Your Quick Start Guide for XML & XSL.

Smart Brain Training Solutions

Copyright © 2016 Smart Brain Training Solutions

All rights reserved.

No part of this publication may be reproduced, stored in a retrieval system or transmitted in any form or by any means, electronic, mechanical, photocopying, recording, scanning or otherwise, except as permitted under Sections 107 and 108 of the 1976 United States Copyright Act, without prior written permission of the Publisher, or authorization through payment of appropriate per-copy fees.

ALL INFORMATION, IDEAS, AND GUIDELINES PRESENTED HEREIN ARE FOR EDUCATIONAL PURPOSES ONLY. THE PUBLISHER AND THE AUTHOR MAKE NO REPRESENTATIONS OR WARRANTIES WITH RESPECT TO THE ACCURACY OR COMPLETENESS OF THE CONTENTS OF THE WORK AND SPECIFICALLY DISCLAIM ALL WARRANTIES, INCLUDING WITHOUT LIMITATION WARRANTIES OF FITNESS FOR A PARTICULAR PURPOSE. IF PROFESSIONAL ASSISTANCE IS NEEDED, THE SERVICES OF A COMPETENT PROFESSIONAL SHOULD BE SOUGHT. NEITHER THE PUBLISHER NOR THE AUTHOR SHALL BE RESPONSIBLE FOR DAMAGES ARISING HEREFROM.

Windows and Windows Server are trademarks of Microsoft corporation. All other trademarks are the property of their respective owners.

Thank you for purchasing *XML & XSL Fast Start*! We hope you'll look for other *Fast Start* guides from Smart Brain Training Solutions.

Table of Contents

1. XML Basics

XML, or eXtensible Markup Language, is a programming language that can be used to describe other languages and a specification for storing information. Although XML and HTML may seem to have a lot in common, in reality the difference between them is like the difference between night and day. HTML is used to format information, but it isn't very useful when it comes to describing information. For example, you can use HTML to format a table, but you can't use HTML to describe the data elements within the table. The reason for this is that you can't really depict something as abstract as a distributor or a customer with HTML, which is where XML comes into the picture. XML can be, and is, used to define the structure of data rather than its format.

What makes XML so powerful is that any type of data—even abstract data concepts—can be given form and structure. You give data concepts—such as distributor, purchase order, and inventory—form by describing their components and the relationship between those components. Instead of the abstract concept of a distributor, you have a specified structure that describes the distributor-related information, such as distributor name, contact name, and address.

You could define the structure of an inventory item handled by the distributor with components such as item number, name, description, unit cost, and suggested retail price.

XML gets this power and versatility from SGML, but it does so without the complexities that make SGML difficult to implement and use on the Web. With this solution, you get the best aspects of SGML without the overhead, which makes XML practical for transmission and use in cyberspace. A key difference between XML and other similar technologies is that XML is used to define the structure of data rather than its format. This means you can use XML to describe the individual data components in a document. For example, using XML you could define the structure of an employee record with components such as employee ID number, full name, contact information, and position within the company. These components could then be further broken down to their basic level.

Although XML can give data structure, you can't use XML to detail how the content is to be rendered. To do this, you have to rely on another technology to format the information. One way to format XML data structures is to combine them with HTML. Here, you create so-called XML islands within standard HTML documents. You use HTML to format the contents of the document, including the data, and you use XML to define the structure of the data. Another formatting solution for XML is to create a style sheet detailing how each piece of the data structure should be formatted. Although a special style sheet language called Extensible Stylesheet Language (XSL) is designed specifically for this purpose, you could also use the cascading style sheet language.

Generally, XML-only documents end with the .xml extension. You can use this extension to tell the application reading the document that it contains XML data. To interpret the data structures within the document, the application relies on an XML processor. Two general types of XML processors are used: those that validate documents and those that don't. A validating XML processor checks the structure of documents; a nonvalidating XML processor doesn't.

> **Note** In practice, XML-only documents created for Web browser display should end with the .xml extension. If you're developing for a different environment, the extension doesn't really matter. The XML parser classes that you use to interpret the document don't need the extension. However, for consistency, it's best to use the .xml extension for files

that contain XML. This ensures that other developers (including yourself at a later date) know what the files contain.

Most XML processors are implemented as extension modules for existing applications. In this context, the XML processor is used within the application to extract information from the XML document and display it in an application window. This window could be in your Web browser or in a stand-alone application.

XML processors are also implemented in programming languages like Java and C#. Here, you use the processor classes to help you extract information from an XML document and display it in an application or applet window.

Tip Another name for a processor is a parser. Not only are there XML parsers, but there are XSL parsers as well. XSL parsers are used to process style sheet definitions in XML documents and render the documents according to those definitions.

2. Using XML

Using XML is a lot easier than you might think. That's because with XML you're in control. Unlike HTML, XML doesn't rely on predefined tags and attributes. This allows you to structure the data in an XML document anyway you like. You define the tags for components within the document. You add attributes to these tags as necessary, and you decide how the components fit together.

The general set of rules for a document's tags and attributes is defined in a document type definition (DTD). XML processors can use the DTD to determine if the document is constructed properly and the processor can pass this information along to the application rendering the document. Keep in mind that documents don't have to have DTDs. However, if they do have a DTD, they should be structured to conform to the DTD.

Once the DTD for a particular type of data is created, you can use the DTD either by inserting it directly into the document, or by referencing the DTD so that it can be imported into the document by the XML processor. Next, you need to create the body of the XML document. There are several ways to do this, and the method you choose depends primarily on how the data is used.

If you're working with fixed data records that change infrequently, you may want to create the necessary data structures using an authoring tool. Here, you insert the data directly into a document and save the result to a file so that it can be viewed directly in an application or compatible browser. You could then publish the document on the Web where others could access it. When you need to update the document, you'd load the document into the authoring tool's editor, make the necessary changes, and then publish the updated document.

If you're working with data that changes frequently, you probably need a more dynamic solution, and rather than creating static documents you could create documents on the fly. To do this, you'd use a document publishing or content management system. These systems are usually integrated with a database. The database stores data records so they can be retrieved on demand. The management system reads in the data and converts it to the appropriate structure based on the DTD and then passes this data off to an application or browser for viewing. Users accessing the dynamic document don't know all this is happening in the background, and they can still access the document using a Uniform Resource Locator (URL).

Extensions to XML

As with most Web technologies, the XML specification is only a starting point. The specification describes XML's core functionality, such as how XML documents are to be defined, and the necessary grammar that enables documents to comply with this definition.

Beyond the core language, several extensions have been defined, including XML Linking Language, XML Pointer Language, Extensible Stylesheet Language (XSL), XML Namespaces, and XML Schema. These technologies are direct extensions of XML that are defined in XML.

Another technology that you'll learn about in this book is XPath. XPath isn't defined in XML—that is, it's a non-XML language. It is, however, a useful technology that is used with XML.

XLink and XPointer

The XML Linking Language (XLink) and the XML Pointer Language (XPointer) are related. XLink defines the relationship between objects—think hypertext reference. XPointer details how to reference specific structures within a document—think internal links within pages. Together, you can use these technologies to create hypertext links for XML documents.

Unlike the simple unidirectional links defined in HTML, XML links are much more sophisticated. Because XML links can be multidirectional, a single XML link can point to multiple resources and you can move through these resources in any order. For example, in an index, a link could point to all references to the word "hypertext" and you could access these resources in any order and then go back to the index using the single link. XML links are also *self-describing*, meaning a link can contain text that describes the resources it relates to.

XSL

XSL provides rich formatting for XML documents. Using XSL, you can define rules that specify how to extract information from an XML document and how to format this information so that it can be viewed. Often, XML data is transformed into another format, such as HTML—as is the case for Microsoft's XSL processor. Because XSL uses XML as its syntax, you don't need to learn yet another markup language.

> **Note** Applications that extract information from XML documents need an XML parser. Applications that extract information from documents and display their contents using XSL style sheets need an XML parser and an XSL parser. While many Web browsers, including Microsoft Internet Explorer, have a built-in XML and XSL parser, applications written in Java or C# must use XML and XSL parser classes to handle the extraction and presentation tasks.

XML Namespaces

XML Namespaces provide easy access to document structures and prevent namespace conflicts within documents that may use like-named structures. By giving each structure a universal name, a document can use markup defined in multiple namespaces, which is pretty cool when you think about it.

XML Schema

With XML Schema, you can create schemas that describe the characteristics of data structures within documents. For example, in the schema you can define how structures are used, how they're grouped together, and how different structures are related. If you're familiar with XML DTDs, you might be thinking that schemas sound a lot like DTDs—and you'd be right. Schemas provide the same functionality as DTDs. However, because XML schemas are written in XML, they're easy to use and completely extensible, making them much more powerful than DTDs.

XPath

XPath is a non-XML language used to identify specific parts of XML documents. Using XPath, you can write expressions that refer to specific structures in a document. These expressions can be used to match and select elements in an input document and copy it into an output document or to process the elements further. XPointer uses the concept of using XPath to identify specific parts of a document to identify the location to which an XLink links. XPath also supports simple arithmetic, string manipulation, and Boolean expressions.

Creating XML-Based Solutions

To create effective XML solutions, developers need many tools. The key tools they may want to use include authoring tools, application development environments, and database and data integration solutions.

Authoring Tools

Creating XML documents isn't easy. Before you get started, you need to decide how to structure data within documents, and, unfortunately, each project typically is different. The reason for this is that the way you might structure inventory data is very different from the way you might structure customer account data. To make matters worse, you may need to define the data structures in a DTD, and DTDs aren't exactly user-friendly.

Enter XML authoring tools, the easy way to define data structures and create documents using those structures. Most XML authoring tools on the market are actually integrated XML/SGML authoring tools. The reason for this is that XML is a subset of SGML and it's very logical to extend existing SGML tools so they're compatible with XML.

Application Development Environments

Application development environments provide a toolkit that can help you implement XML solutions. Because most of these toolkits come complete with XML parsers, conversion utilities, and more, you can be sure that you'll be able to start and finish an XML-based project.

Database and Data Integration Solutions

Databases can use XML to structure information extracted from the database so that it can be distributed and published. Data integration solutions take this concept a few steps further by using XML to automate the exchange of data. Generally speaking, with an integration solution XML serves as an interface layer or wrapper for data being passed between data sources. This makes it possible for a wide variety of applications, legacy systems, and databases to exchange information.

XML Document Structure

XML documents, like Hypertext Markup Language (HTML) documents, contain text and can be written using any text editor or word processor, such as Microsoft Notepad. For ease of reference, XML documents normally are saved with the .xml extension. The .xml extension ensures that the document is easily recognized as containing XML and that applications, such as Microsoft Internet Explorer, view the document as such.

XML documents are built using text content marked up with tags. For a document describing items in an inventory, these tags could be <item>, <item_number>, <item_name>, and <item_description>. In addition to tags, XML documents can contain other types of markup, including attributes, processing instructions, entity references, comments, and character data. Each of these types of markup is discussed in this text.

XML Naming Rules

XML uses the same building blocks as HTML. Because of this, XML documents can contain elements, attributes, and values. Elements are the most basic parts of XML documents. They can contain other elements and text.

The names of elements, attributes, and other structures in XML must conform to a specific naming convention. They may include alphanumeric characters, which include the letters a-z and A-Z as well as the numerals 0-9, in addition to non-English letters, numbers, and ideograms. They may also include three punctuation characters:

- Underscore (_)
- Hyphen (-)
- Period (.)

> **Note** The only other punctuation character allowed in the names for XML structures is colon (:). The colon character is reserved for XML namespaces.

Names for XML structures may not contain white space, and they may not begin with a hyphen, a period or a number. They may, however, begin with the English letters A to Z, ideograms, and the underscore character. This means that while the following are invalid element names:

```
<.inventory></.inventory>
< item26></ item26>
<product^inventory></product^inventory>
```

The following are valid names:

```
<_inventory></_inventory>
<item26></item26>
<product-inventory></product-inventory>
```

3. Working with Root, Parent, and Child Elements

XML documents are processed a bit differently than other types of documents. With XML, documents should be structured as a tree that processors can navigate easily using method or function calls. Because of this, every XML document has a root element, which is the basis or starting point of the tree hierarchy.

Understanding Root Elements

The root element is the first element in a document, and it contains all other elements. In the following example, `inventory` is the root element and all other elements are contained within it:

```
<inventory>
  <item tracking_number="459323" manufacturer="Not
listed">
    <item_type>Oak Nightstand</item_type>
    <description>Single-drawer nightstand. Solid
oak.</description>
  </item>
  <item tracking_number="459789" manufacturer="Not
listed">
    <item_type>Oak Desk</item_type>
    <description>Writer's desk with large drawer.
Solid oak.</description>
  </item>
</inventory>
```

Every well-formed XML document has one, and only one, root element. In the example, the inventory element is the parent of the item elements. That is, the inventory element contains the item elements. Every element, except the root element, has exactly one parent element.

Understanding Parent and Child Elements

Parent elements, such as the item elements in the previous example, can contain other elements. These elements are called child elements. In the previous example, the child elements of item are item_type and description. Tags at the same level in a tree hierarchy, such as item_type and description, are referred to as siblings.

Nesting Parent and Child Elements

In XML you can't overlap tags. The opening and ending tags of child elements must be inside the parent element and can't overlap with the tags of siblings.

The following code is improperly formatted:

```
<item>
  <item_type><description>Oak Nightstand
  </item_type></description>
</item>
```

To properly format the example, the item_type and description elements can't overlap. This means the code should be written as:

```
<item>
  <item_type>Oak Nightstand</item_type>
  <description></description>
</item>
```

Adding Root Elements to Documents

To add a root element to a document, follow these steps:

1. Open an XML document for editing, or create a new document.

2. At the beginning of the document, type **<name>**, where *name* is the name of the element that will contain the rest of the elements in the document. The name must conform to the XML naming rules discussed in the previous section.

3. Enter other structures as necessary (using the techniques discussed later in this text).

4. Type **</name>**, ensuring that *name* exactly matches the name used in Step 2.

> **Note** While no other elements are allowed outside the root element, other XML structures, such as processing instructions and schemas, can be placed before the start of the root element. You'll find a discussion of processing instructions later in this text.

4. Defining XML Elements and Tags

XML has no predefined elements. You can create any elements you like in XML documents. In most cases you use element names that identify the content and make it easier to process the information later. XML elements are written in one of two forms; either with beginning and ending tags, or as empty tags. Each form can have a special meaning.

The sections that follow examine the key element types and how elements are used in XML documents.

Using Elements Tag Pairs

All elements have an opening tag and an ending tag. In the opening tag, the element name is written between less than (<) and greater than (>) signs, such as <item>. In the ending tag, the element name is written between a less than symbol followed by a slash (</) and a greater than (>) sign. For example, inventory item could have an opening tag of <item> and an ending tag of </item>.

> **Note** XML is used to define data structures and not formatting. With this in mind, it's important to remember that the names of XML elements reflect the type of content inside the element and not how that content will be formatted on the screen.

Everything between an element's opening tag and its ending tag is the element's content. In a document the item element could be used as follows:

```
<item>Oak Nightstand</item>
```

Here, the element's content is the text string:

```
Oak Nightstand
```

Although any white space between the opening and ending tag is part of the content, most applications, including Web browsers, choose to ignore it. This means the element content's could be entered into the document as:

```
<item>
Oak Nightstand
</item>
```

or even:

```
<item>
     Oak Nightstand
</item>
```

and it'll be handled the same way. In the example, <item> and </item> are markup and the text string Oak Nightstand—and any white space around it—is character data.

The only characters you can't use in content are the less than symbol (<) and the ampersand symbol (&). These characters are reserved by XML and must not be used as part of the normal text in a document. Instead of using the < or & symbol, you must use an escaped value called a *predefined entity reference*. When an XML parse sees this escape value, it replaces the value with the actual character. (For more information, see the section of Chapter 6 entitled "Using Predefined Entity References.")

Unlike HTML, XML is case-sensitive. This means that you must enter elements in the same case throughout a document or set of documents and that the case must match the one used in a document's document type definition (DTD)—if one is provided. For example, if you defined an element called employee, the matching tags are <employee> and </employee>. The opening tags

<Employee> and <EMPLOYEE> would refer to different elements, as would the ending tags </Employee> and </EMPLOYEE>.

> **Tip** Although you can't start a tag using one case, such as <employee>, and end with a different case, such as </Employee>, you can use lower, upper, or mixed cases in element names. The key is that the case must be consistent within any one element.

To add an element with beginning and ending tags to a document, follow these steps:

1. Open an XML document for editing. If the document doesn't have a root element, add one following the steps outlined in Chapter 3 "Working with Root, Parent, and Child Elements." Afterward, move the insertion point after the opening tag for the root element, making sure to follow the nesting rules as appropriate.

2. Type the opening tag for the element you want to specify, such as <item>. Be sure to follow the naming rules defined in the section of Chapter 2 entitled "XML Naming Rules."

3. Enter any content after the opening tag, such as descriptive text. Afterward, enter the ending tag for the element, such as </item>. The name must match exactly the name used previously.

Using Empty Elements

Not all elements have content. In XML you can define an element without content as an *empty element*. Unlike other elements that have an opening and ending tag, empty elements only have a opening tag, which is specially formatted to indicate that no ending element follows.

Empty elements begin with the less than symbol (<) and end with a slash followed by a greater than symbol (/>). For example, you could write a symbol element as <symbol />. Writing <symbol /> is the same as writing <symbol></symbol>.

In XML you can, in fact, use either technique to write empty elements. You can't, however, write only an opening or ending tag. Doing so would result in the document being improperly structured.

Empty elements can be created as top-level elements just below the root element in the tree hierarchy or as child elements of existing elements. As with other types of elements, empty elements must be properly nested. This means that you could use:

```
<employee>
   <name first="Ted" initial="H" last="Green" />
   <id empnum="123" />
</employee>
```

or

```
<employee>
   <name first="Ted" initial="H" last="Green"></name>
   <id empnum="123"></id>
</employee>
```

However, you could not use:

```
<employee>
   <name first="Ted" initial="H" last="Green">
   </id empnum="123">
</employee>
```

or

```
<employee>
   <name first="Ted" initial="H" last="Green">
   <id empnum="123">
</employee>
</name></id>
```

To add an empty element with a single tag to a document, follow these steps:

1. Open an XML document for editing and then move the insertion point to where you want to insert the empty element. Be sure to follow the proper nesting rules.

2. Type the element you want to specify using the form <name />, such as <item />. Be sure to follow the naming rules defined in the section Chapter 2 entitled "XML Naming Rules."

To add an empty element with separate opening and ending tags to a document, follow these steps:

1. Open an XML document for editing and then move the insertion point to where you want to insert the empty element. Be sure to follow the proper nesting rules.

2. Type the opening tag for the element you want to specify, such as <item>.

3. Immediately after the opening tag, enter the ending tag for the element, such as </item>.

5. Using XML Attributes

As with elements, attributes are an important part of XML documents. You use attributes to describe characteristics of the data structure you're building.

Defining Attributes

Attributes, which can be contained within an element's opening tag, have quotation-mark delimited values that further describe the data structure that the element represents. For example, the item element could have an attribute called tracking_number, which serves as a tracking number for each item in the inventory. If the tracking number for an Oak Nightstand were 459323, then you could write the item element with the attribute as:

```
<item tracking_number="459323">
Oak Nightstand
</item>
```

> **Note** The equals sign is being used to assign the value to the attribute. The value assigned to the attribute can have white space around the equals sign. Here, the white space would be added purely to make the value easier to read when viewed in a text editor.

Because either single quotation marks or double quotation marks are acceptable, the element could also be written as:

```
<item tracking_number='459323'>
Oak Nightstand
</item>
```

> **Tip** Switching between single quotation marks and double quotation marks is required when the attribute value itself contains either single or double quotation marks. If an attribute value contained single quotation marks, you could use double quotation marks to enclose it. If an attribute value contained double quotation marks, you could use single quotation marks to enclose it.

As shown in the previous examples, attribute values are defined using text strings enclosed by quotation marks. As with element content, attribute values may not use the less than symbol (<) or the ampersand (&). Instead, you should replace these values with the appropriate predefined entity reference. Predefined entity references are also provided for single and double quotation marks to eliminate any confusion that may be caused by having quotation marks inside attribute values.

Elements can have multiple attributes, provided that each attribute has a unique name. If you need to specify an attribute several times, you'll need to create separate elements. For example, you'd write:

```
<employee>
  <name first="Ted" initial="H" last="Green" />
  <job role="contractor" />
  <job role="sales" />
</employee>
```

instead of:

```
<employee>
  <name first="Ted" initial="H" last="Green" />
  <job role="contractor" role="sales" />
</employee>
```

When To Use Attributes

Because both elements and attributes can be used to hold information, you may be wondering which to use when. For example, it's better to write:

```
<item>
  <item_type>Oak Nightstand</item_type>
  <tracking_number>459323</tracking_number>
  <manufacturer>Not listed</manufacturer>
  <description>
   Single-drawer nightstand. Solid oak.
   </description>
</item>
```

or

```
<item tracking_number="459323" manufacturer="Not
listed">
  <item_type>Oak Nightstand</item_type>
  <description>
   Single-drawer nightstand. Solid oak.
   </description>
</item>
```

Unfortunately, there's no clear answer, and different people would have different arguments as to which is correct. Officially, attributes are name-value pairs used with elements (that can contain information about the data or contain actual data). Still, there are some who argue that information contained in attributes is metadata, meaning it's only information about the data rather than being data itself. In the school of thought where attribute values are metadata, you could have attributes, such as lang, used to describe the language used for the element's content, but you wouldn't have attributes that contained actual values, such as an item's description or type.

As you set out to use attributes in XML, you'll probably find that it's better to think of attribute values as both metadata and data. In this way you can use an attribute in a way that makes sense for a specific situation rather than being tied to one school of thought.

You'll often find that the application you're using to display the data will help determine how attributes are used. In some cases applications may be able to process attribute values more easily than they can process the raw contents of elements. In other cases you may want to hide certain types of information from viewers until they perform a specific action that causes the values to be displayed or processed.

Adding Attributes to Elements

Attributes specify additional information for data structures. Elements can have zero or more attributes. The order of attributes doesn't matter as long as the attributes are entered before the closing > of the opening tag.

To add an attribute to an element, follow these steps:

1. After the name of the element in the opening tag and before the closing >, type **attribute=** where *attribute* is the name of the attribute you're adding to the tag. Each attribute name for a given element must be unique. If the element already has an attribute of the same name, the name used for the new attribute must be different.

2. Specify the value for the attribute using either single or double quotation marks, such as "value" or 'value'.

> **Note** Either form of quotation marks is acceptable, as long as the same type of quotation mark is used at the beginning and ending of the value. If the value contains a double quotation mark, however, you should enclose the value in single

quotation marks. Similarly, if the value contains a single quotation mark, you should enclose the value in double quotation marks.

6. Additional Structures in Elements

In addition to defining elements, attributes, and values, XML documents can contain entity references, character data sections, comments, and processing instructions. These structures are examined in the sections that follow.

Using Predefined Entity References

Entity references are placeholders for other values or other types of content. XML predefines several entity references that allow you to enter text containing characters that are otherwise reserved in the language or that may be misinterpreted.

The two reserved characters in the language are the less than symbol (<) and the ampersand symbol (&). Characters that can easily be misinterpreted are the greater than symbol (>), the single quotation mark ('), and the double quotation mark ("). This means there are five predefined entity references:

- **<** The less than symbol; reserved for the opening bracket of elements.

- **>** The greater than symbol; normally used for the closing bracket of elements.

- **&** The ampersand symbol; reserved to specify the beginning of an entity reference.

- **"** The straight, double quotation mark; normally used to enclose attribute values.

- **'** The apostrophe or straight single quotation mark; normally used to enclose attribute values.

> **Note**   is not a predefined entity for XML. However, this entity frequently is used in HTML to force whitespace characters. To use this character in XML without resulting in an error, you have to use the actual character code, such as ** **, or define the   entity yourself in the DTD.

You can use the predefined entity references as part of an elements content, as shown here:

```
<business>J. Henry &amp; Associates</business>
```

With attributes, you can use predefined entity references, as shown here:

```
<business name="J. Henry &amp;
Associates"></business>
```

Entity references, such as " and ', are considered to be markup. When an application processes an XML document containing these references, it replaces the entity reference with the actual character to which it refers. This means that in both cases, J. Henry & Associates is replaced with Green & Associates when it's displayed.

To add an entity reference to a document, follow these steps:

1. Open an XML document for editing and then locate the text that contains a value you need to replace with an entity reference or move the pointer to the position where the value should be inserted.

2. Delete the character you're replacing (if any) and then type the entity reference you want to use, such as &.

Using Character Data Sections

Character data sections allow you to specify areas within an XML document that contain raw character data and aren't to be processed by XML parsers. You'll find that character data sections are useful when you want to include XML, HTML, or other examples containing markup in a document without replacing all the reserved or possibly misinterpreted values with entity references. You can, for example, insert an entire snippet of markup within a character data section.

Character data sections have beginning and ending designators. The beginning designator is <![CDATA[and the ending designator is]]>. Everything within these designators is handled as raw character data and isn't processed. This means the & and < characters can appear within the character data section and they won't be interpreted as markup. The only value that can't appear within a character data section is the end designator]]>.

Here's an example of a character data section in an XML document:

```
<book title="101 Great Golf Destinations">
  <chapter number="3" title="Seaside Golf Resorts">
    <page>
      <![CDATA[ <p> A text paragraph </p>
               <br /> for line breaks
               <hr /> for horizontal rules
      ]]>
    </page>
    <main_text></main_text>
  </chapter>
</book>
```

Character data sections can appear anywhere in a document, as long as they're between the opening and ending tags for the root element. To add a character data section to an XML document, follow these steps:

1. Open an XML document for editing and then move the pointer to the position where the character data section should be inserted.

2. Type <![CDATA[.

3. Enter the text containing markup or other structures that you want to display but don't want to be parsed.

4. Type]]>.

> **Note** The only use for the]]> designator is to end the character data section. Although this prevents you from nesting character data sections within other character data sections, you can insert multiple character data sections into a single document. To do this, you must start and end one section before beginning another section.

Using Comments

Comments are useful in any programming or markup language, and XML is no exception. You can use comments to annotate sections of an XML document or to add general notes for the XML document overall. As with HTML, XML comments begin with <!-- and with -->. Here's an example:

```
<!-- Still working to get the example structures in
correct sequence -->
```

No spaces are required between the double hyphens and the comment text. This allows you to write:

```
<!--Still working to get the example structures in
correct sequence-->
```

The double hyphen can't appear anywhere else within the comment text. This prevents you from writing:

```
<!-- Still working -- example structures aren't in
correct sequence -->
```

and

```
<!-- Still working on example structures --->
```

Comments are best used to specify information that may be useful to other document authors as they set out to work with a document. Comments aren't displayed in applications, such as Internet Explorer, by default but can be viewed if the document's source code is available. However, a document's parsed contents may or may not contain the hidden comments. The reason for this is that XML parsers may choose to ignore the comments and not pass them along with the document's contents.

> **Note** You shouldn't rely on comments being available in an application. If you need to pass on information in a document, you may want to use processing instructions. Processing instructions provide special instructions or additional information to the application rendering a document.

Because comments aren't parsed, they can occur anywhere in the text of a document. This means they could occur before the opening root tag or after the ending root tag as well. To add a comment to a document, follow these steps:

1. Open an XML document for editing and then move the pointer to the position where the comment should be inserted.

2. Type <!--.

3. Enter the text for the comment.

4. Type -->.

Using Processing Instructions

Processing instructions are used to pass information to applications. The application processing the document can use the instructions to perform special tasks or simply as a source of additional information regarding a document.

Processing instructions begin with <? and end with ?>. The most commonly used processing instructions are those that specify a style sheet attached to a document and those that set the XML version, encoding, and mode for a document. An example instruction that sets a style sheet is:

```
<?xml-stylesheet href="corp.css" type="text/css"?>
```

An example of a processing instruction that sets version, encoding, and mode follows:

```
<?xml version="1.1" encoding="US-ASCII"
standalone="yes"?>
```

Documents don't have to have either type of processing instruction. However, if they do, certain rules apply:

- If a document has a processing instruction that specifies a style sheet, the style sheet is used to format elements in the document. When multiple style sheets are used, the style sheet definitions applied last take precedence over those applied earlier. If you don't declare style definitions for every element in the document, the default font settings are applied.

- If a document has a processing instruction that declares the XML version, encoding, and mode, the instruction must be the first line of the document. It can't be preceded by comments, white space, or other processing instructions. (For more information on this type of instruction, see the following section, "Specifying XML Declarations.")

To add a processing instruction to a document, follow these steps:

1. Open an XML document for editing and then move the pointer to the position where the processing instruction should be inserted.

2. Type <?.

3. Type the instruction name immediately after the open instruction tag, such as **<?xml** or **<?xml-stylesheet**. Don't use a space between the instruction name and the start of the tag.

4. Enter the body of the instruction.

5. Type **?>**.

7. Specifying XML Declarations

An XML declaration is a processing instruction that sets the version, encoding, and mode for an XML document. Declarations aren't required in documents. However, as stated previously, if they're present, they must be the first line of the document and they must not be preceded by comments, white space, or other processing instructions.

XML declarations can specify three attributes: version, encoding, and standalone, as shown in the following example:

```
<?xml version="1.0" encoding="ISO-8859_1"
standalone="yes"?>
```

These attributes have special meaning and are discussed in the sections that follow.

Using the Version Attribute

The version attribute in an XML declaration sets the version of XML used in the document. In use versions of XML include version 1.0 and version 1.1.

If you use an XML declaration, the version attribute is mandatory. The other attributes, however, are optional. Because of this, the following XML declaration is valid:

```
<?xml version="1.0"?>
```

As is:

```
<?xml version="1.1"?>
```

Using the Encoding Attribute

XML parsers assume documents are encoded using either UTF-8 or UTF-16. UTF is the Unicode Transformation Format. Because UTF-8 allows variable length characters, parsers use the first few characters in a document to deduce the number of bytes used to express characters. If necessary, you can set the document encoding using the optional encoding attribute for an XML declaration. In the following example the encoding is ISO-8859 Latin 1:

```
<?xml version="1.0" encoding="ISO-8859_1"?>
```

If a document is written in UTF-8 or UTF-16, the document encoding can be omitted. When any other encoding is specified, the parser reading the document translates characters from the document's native encoding (as set in the encoding attribute of the XML declaration) into Unicode.

UTF-8 and UTF-16 are implementations of the international standard character set, Unicode. XML parsers are required to support both the UTF-8 and UTF-16 implementations of Unicode. Support for other character encoding is optional. Nevertheless, the recommended set of supported encoding includes:

EUC-JP   ISO-8859-4

ISO-10646-UCS-2   ISO-8859-5

ISO-10646-UCS-4   ISO-8859-6

ISO-2022-JP   ISO-8859-7

ISO-8859-1   ISO-8859-8

ISO-8859-2   ISO-8859-9

ISO-8859-3

Using the Standalone Attribute

The standalone attribute in an XML declaration sets the mode for the document and is optional. You can use two values:

- **standalone="no"** If standalone is set to *no*, the document may have to read an external DTD to determine the validity of the document's structures and to determine values for parts of the document that use entities or other references defined in the DTD.

- **standalone="yes"** If standalone is set to *yes*, the document doesn't rely on an external DTD. This doesn't mean the document doesn't have a DTD. The document and may have an internally specified DTD. (For more information on DTDs, see Part II "DTDs and Namespaces").

When the standalone attribute isn't set in the XML declaration, the value standalone="no" is assumed. This allows the parser to retrieve a DTD if one is referenced.

8. Creating Well-Formed Documents

Regardless of whether XML documents have a DTD, they must be well-formed. If a document is well-formed, it can be said that the document conforms to specific rules of the XML specification, including these rules:

- A document must have exactly one root element.

- Every start tag must have a matching end tag (or use the empty element format).

- Elements can't be nested improperly so that they overlap.

- Attribute values must be enclosed within single or double quotation marks.

- Attribute names within elements must be unique; elements can't have two attributes with the same name.

- Unescaped < and & signs can't appear as part of an element's content or as part of an attribute's value.

- Comments and processing instructions can't appear inside tags.

Although the list isn't exhaustive, you can see that there are many rules that determine whether a document is well-formed. The most basic well-formed document is one that contains a single element, such as:

```
<inventory>
  100 Oak Nightstands
</inventory>
```

This basic document can be read and understood by XML parsers. It meets all the constraints of the previous rules. However, most documents you'll work with will be considerably more complex and it'll be much more difficult to determine if the document is well-formed. In fact, if you create an XML document by hand, you can almost be assured that it'll contain some type of well-formedness error.

One way to determine if a document is well-formed is to load the document into a Web browser that includes an XML parser, such as Internet Explorer. If there are problems with the document, the browser should display an error message. As you correct each error, additional errors may be displayed when you reload the document.

When the document is finally free of errors, the document should load into the browser and display using the default style sheet. Of course, using Internet Explorer to check documents isn't the most sophisticated technique you can use. If you are a programmer, you can use the parser classes from an application programming interface (API), such as Java or C#.

9. Understanding DTDs

To ensure that not only are the data structures in the documents formatted correctly, but also that the documents can be understood by the applications that will process them, you need a way of expressing the necessary data structures as a set of rules and ensuring conformity. What you need is a custom application of XML, which is why document type definitions (DTDs) and schemas are used.

Both DTDs and schemas allow you to create XML applications. An XML application defines a custom markup language that describes specific types of data and uses the rules set out in the associated DTD or schema. The DTD/schema rules specify items that are allowed or required in compliant documents. Once you create an XML application using a DTD or schema, you can write documents that conform to your custom markup language. Application software, database systems, and other programs can use the DTD/schema to interpret compliant documents and ensure conformity to the rule set.

DTDs have a formal—fairly rigid—syntax that precisely describes the elements and entities that may appear in a document, as well as the contents and attributes for acceptable elements. In a DTD you could specify that a purchase order must have one and only one order number but can have one or more requested products. You could go on to specify that each purchase order must have one order date and one customer identifier but no more. These details in the DTD would allow programs to determine if purchase orders are valid.

Validity is an important concept when DTDs are used. If a document is valid, it can be said that it conforms to its DTD. If a document is invalid, the document doesn't conform to its DTD. However, keep in mind that validation is an optional step in processing XML. Programs that use validating parsers can compare documents to their DTD and list places where the document differs from the DTD specification. The programs can then determine actions to take regarding noncompliance with the DTD. Some programs may mark the document as invalid and stop processing it. Other programs may try to correct problems in the document and reprocess it.

Although DTDs can help you specify constraints for documents, DTDs don't specify every nuance of a document's format. Among other things, a DTD doesn't control allowed values, the denotation of elements (explicit meaning), the connotation of elements (figurative meaning), or the character data that can be associated with elements. This allows for flexibility in the document structure so that you can create many types of documents using the same set of rules.

All valid documents include a reference to the DTD to which they conform. DTDs aren't mandatory, however. When a document lacks a DTD, the XML processor can't verify that the data format is appropriate, but it can still attempt to interpret the data.

> **Note...** A document that is well-formed but doesn't have a DTD wouldn't be considered valid. The reason for this is that the document doesn't have a DTD, and, as a result, the document can't be said to comply with the DTD. The document, however, is still a well-formed XML document.

DTDs can be specified in several different ways. An internal DTD is one that is defined within a document. An external DTD is one that is defined in a separate document and is imported into the document. Both types of DTDs have their advantages and disadvantages.

Internal DTDs are convenient when you want to apply constraints to an individual document and then easily distribute the document along with its DTD. They're also convenient when you're developing a complex DTD and want to test an example document against the

DTD. Putting the DTD and the related markup in the same file makes it easy to modify the DTD and the example document as often as necessary during testing.

With an external DTD, you place a reference to a DTD in a file rather than the DTD itself. This makes it easy to apply the DTD to multiple documents. Because the DTD is referenced rather than included, you can make changes to the DTD later and you don't need to edit the DTD definition in each and every document to which it's applied. Two types of external DTDs are used:

- Public Public DTDs are DTDs that have been standardized and provide a publicly available set of rules for writing specific types of XML documents, such as those used by the airlines or insurance industries.
- Nonpublic Nonpublic DTDs are DTDs created by private organizations or individuals. Generally speaking, these DTDs aren't publicly available (or haven't become a public standard).

When you use an external DTD, you should set the standalone attribute of the XML declaration to no, such as:

```
<?xml version="1.0" encoding="US-ASCII"
standalone="no"?>
```

> **Tip** Validating parsers are required to read the external DTD you specify when you set standalone to no. Nonvalidating parsers, however, may read the external DTD but aren't required to—even if standalone is set to no. This is important to Note... because a nonvalidating parser that reads an external DTD would be able to replace DTD-defined entity references with their actual values. However, a nonvalidating parser that doesn't read an external DTD wouldn't know what to do with DTD-defined entity references that occur in a document. To improve parsing times, developers sometimes set standalone to yes so that external DTDs aren't read. If you choose not to read an

> external DTD, you should be certain that the DTD doesn't contain definitions (such as entity references) that are needed in the document.

You specify DTDs using the DOCTYPE assignment. The DOCTYPE assignment is one of the most basic elements in an XML document. Similar to the document type element, which is a container for all other elements, the DOCTYPE declaration is a container for all DTD assignments.

Using Elements in DTDs

Every element used in a valid document must be declared in the document's document type definition (DTD). Element declarations specify the markup tags that can appear in a conforming document and how those tags can be used. If a DTD doesn't declare elements that are used in a document, the document can't be said to be valid.

> **Note** Keep in mind that XML is case sensitive. This means you must use the exact case for keywords and declarations specified. There are no exceptions.

Five types of elements are used in XML documents:

- Those with standard content
- Those with only character data
- Those with mixed content
- Those with any type of content allowed
- Those with no content allowed

You declare each of these element types using the ELEMENT declaration, which consists of an element name followed by a description of the element's contents in the form:

```
<!ELEMENT element_name (element_content)>
```

where element_name is the name of the element and element_content specifies the child elements, text, or both, that the element will contain. If an element declaration has contents, those contents are always enclosed in the opening and closing parentheses. I'll discuss the exceptions shortly.

Each and every element that you allow in the body of an XML document must be declared. Techniques for declaring the various types of elements are discussed in the sections that follow.

> **Note...** The name of an element can be any legal XML name, as discussed in the section of Chapter 2 entitled "XML Naming Rules." This means you could name an element describing purchase orders as purchase-order, purchase_order, or purchase.order. Once it's declared in the DTD, you could use the element describing purchase orders in the body of the XML document.

Using Attributes in DTDs

Like HTML elements, XML elements can have attributes. Because a document's elements are completely configurable, you're free to create as many attributes as necessary. However, all attributes used in a valid document must be declared in the document type definition (DTD). Otherwise the document can't be said to be valid.

You define a list of attributes for an element with the ATTLIST assignment. Using the ATTLIST assignment, you could declare a shipping attribute for the purchase_order element used previously like this:

```
<!ATTLIST purchase_order shipping CDATA #REQUIRED>
```

This declaration says the shipping attribute is required and contains character data.

You can assign multiple attributes to an element using a single assignment as well. In the following example, shipping, prepaid, and type are defined as possible attributes for the purchase_order element:

```
<!ATTLIST purchase_order shipping CDATA #REQUIRED
          prepaid CDATA #REQUIRED
          type  CDATA #REQUIRED
>
```

The declaration specifies that the shipping, prepaid, and type attributes are required. It also specifies that the attributes contain character data. The spacing used in the example is added for readability and isn't required. You could also have entered:

```
<!ATTLIST purchase_order shipping CDATA #REQUIRED
prepaid CDATA #REQUIRED
type CDATA #REQUIRED>
```

or you could have used a separate attribute declaration for each attribute, such as:

```
<!ATTLIST purchase_order shipping CDATA #REQUIRED>
<!ATTLIST purchase_order prepaid CDATA #REQUIRED>
<!ATTLIST purchase_order type  CDATA #REQUIRED>
```

As you can see from the examples, the ATTLIST assignment uses the following syntax:

```
<!ATTLIST element_describing attrib_name attrib_type
default_usage>
```

What this means is that when you create attributes, you must complete the following steps:

1. Start the assignment by typing **<!ATTLIST**.

2. Specify the element the attribute relates to. In previous examples this is purchase_order.

3. Give the attribute a name. In the examples the attributes are named shipping, prepaid, and type.

> **Note...** Attribute names must be valid XML names, meaning that they must conform to the XML naming rules discussed in Chapter 2.

4. Set the attribute type, such as CDATA or ENTITY.

5. Set the default usage, such as #REQUIRED or #FIXED.

6. Complete the assignment by typing >.

10. Introducing XSL

Extensible Stylesheet Language (XSL) defines rules that specify how to extract information from an XML document and how to format this information so that it can be viewed. XSL is divided into several parts and includes:

- **XSL Transformations (XSLT)** A language for transforming XML documents
- **XML Path (XPath)** An expression language used by XSLT to access and refer to parts of a document
- **XSL Formatting Objects (XSL-FO)** An XML vocabulary used by XSLT to describe the formatting of text on a page

XSLT is a language for transforming XML documents. You use XSLT to specify the rules by which one XML document is transformed into another type of document. Although the output of the transformation process could be an XML document, it's more commonly an HTML document that's designed to be viewed by users. The output could also be a Unicode text file, a Portable Document File (PDF), a file containing programming code written in Java, Active Server Pages (ASP) or another programming language, or just about any other file type.

The typical transformation process starts with an input document that's matched against a set of one or more XSLT documents, called XSLT stylesheets. You write XSLT stylesheets to define the rules for transforming a specific type of XML document. During the transformation process, an XSLT processor analyzes the contents of the input document to match specific criteria defined in the stylesheet. These criteria are organized as templates that define actions to take when a match is found. When an XSLT processor determines that an element matches a template definition, it writes the contents of the template to an output buffer. Upon finishing the analysis, the processor might restructure the output buffer to format the document as XML, HTML, and so on.

XSLT is created to be more powerful and versatile than other stylesheet languages, such as cascading style sheets (CSS). Although you can use CSS with XML, it really isn't optimized to work with data. You can use CSS to specify font types, set margins, and position content, but you can't use CSS to perform many of the tasks you'll want to perform on data. Tasks that XSLT excels at include

- **Sorting** Allows you to change the order of elements according to a set of criteria. For example, you could sort a list of accounts alphabetically.
- **Filtering** Allows you to remove elements that aren't applicable in a specific context. For example, you could filter out incomplete orders from an order summary to show only orders that have been completed.
- **Calculating** Allows you to perform arithmetic functions. For example, you could total the sales proceeds from multiple orders.
- **Merging** Allows you to combine multiple documents into a single document. For example, you could combine all the sales orders for the month into a single summary document called Monthly Sales.

When you need to perform any of these tasks on data or perform standard transformations going from XML to another format, XSLT should be your tool of choice. Don't worry, if you need to apply formatting to a document after it's been transformed, you can still do this—I'll show you how later in this text.

Because a solid understanding of the transformation process is essential to working with XSLT, lets take a more detailed look at this process, starting with the following sample input document:

```
<?xml version="1.0"?>
```

```
<document>
XSLT is a powerful transformation language.
</document>
```

Although you can view an XML document directly in a Web browser or another application, the document isn't formatted. To format the document for viewing, you'd want to transform the document into another format, such as HTML. Here's an XSLT stylesheet that specifies how to transform the sample document:

```
<xsl:stylesheet version="2.0"
  xmlns:xsl="http://www.w3.org/1999/XSL/Transform">

  <xsl:output method="html"/>

  <xsl:template match="/">
    <xsl:apply-templates select="document"/>
  </xsl:template>

  <xsl:template match="document">
    <html>
      <body>
        <p>
          <xsl:value-of select="."/>
        </p>
      </body>
    </html>
  </xsl:template>

</xsl:stylesheet>
```

> **Tip** All markup inserted into an XSLT stylesheet must be well formed, regardless of whether the markup is XML, HTML, or some other markup language. Thus, although HTML would allow you to enter only the opening paragraph tag <p>, you must enter both the opening and closing paragraph tags.

Although I'll examine XSLT stylesheets in detail shortly, let's focus on the basics for now. The first template in this stylesheet tells an XSLT processor to find the root element and apply the second template to any `document` elements in the source document. The second template replaces the begin <document> and end </document> tags with the HTML markup provided and then inserts the value of the `document` element into the HTML paragraph tag.

The result is the following HTML document:

```
<html>
<body>
<p>
   XSLT is a powerful transformation language.
</p>
</body>
</html>
```

As with XML processors, you can find a number of capable XSLT processors. Once you've installed a processor, you can use the processes to parse and transform documents. After you've transformed a file into a specific format, you can view the file in an appropriate application, such as a Web browser, to ensure that the transformation worked.

When working with XSLT, keep in mind that the only template automatically applied to any document is the template for the root node. All other templates must be invoked when a particular document structure matches a template rule. You must explicitly define expressions to determine which additional templates are applied. You do this by defining a root template that in turn invokes other templates.

Templates are always recursively processed. In this example the root template specifies that there are templates for three elements (`element1`, `element2`, and `element3`):

```
<xsl:stylesheet version="2.0"
   xmlns:xsl="http://www.w3.org/1999/XSL/Transform">

   <xsl:template match="/">
```

```
      <xsl:apply-templates select="element1"/>
      <xsl:apply-templates select="element2"/>
      <xsl:apply-templates select="element3"/>
   </xsl:template>
...
</xsl:stylesheet>
```

The XSLT processor would start with the root template and then process the template for element1. If the rules for element1 invoked other templates, these templates would each be processed in turn. When the processor was finished recursively processing templates associated with element1, the processor would start with the rules for element2, and so on.

11. Matching Structures to Template Rules

Recursion is a powerful aspect of XSLT. When XSLT processors analyze input documents, they see document structures as node trees, where nodes represent individual pieces of the XML document, such as elements, attributes, text, comments, and processing instructions, and the node tree itself is a hierarchical representation of the entire XML document.

At the top of the node tree is the root node, which represents a document's root element. Top-level elements in a document become branches of the tree with the low-level elements that they contain below them. Any contents or attributes of elements are broken out in the tree structure as well. This makes the node tree easy to traverse as long as the processor understands the basic parent-child-sibling concepts used with XSLT and knows how to locate various types of nodes using these concepts.

The actual underlying technology that enables document structures to be represented as node trees and traversed is XPath. XPath defines a set of standard nodes and provides the functions for locating those nodes. Node types defined by XPath are

- **Root** Represents the root element in XML documents (each document has only one root node). The root node contains the entire document. Although it has no parent nodes, all top-level nodes are its children and all nodes are its descendants.
- **Element** Represents all elements in XML documents, including root nodes. This means that element nodes exist for the root element and all other elements in a document. Elements nodes can have parents and children. The parent nodes are either the root node or another higher-level element node. Children nodes

can include other element nodes, text nodes, comment nodes, and processing instruction nodes that occur within the element.

- **Attribute** Represents attributes in XML documents. Although element nodes are the parent of attribute nodes, attribute nodes aren't children of element nodes. This is a subtle but important semantic distinction between attribute nodes and other nodes. The reason for this distinction is that attribute nodes aren't present unless they're specifically requested. Once an attribute is requested, a node is added to the node tree and the value of the attribute can be read. This remains true if default values for attributes are defined in a document type definition (DTD) or schema but aren't explicitly specified in elements. Attributes inherited by an element from higher-level elements are also available. This applies to the xml:lang and xml:space attributes, which are applied to an element and inherited by its child elements. Keep in mind that the XML processor must be able to access external DTDs or schemas to determine that default values are defined and available. If the processor can't do this, the default values won't be available.

- **Text** Represents the text contents of elements. If any text associated with an element contains entity or character references, these references are resolved before the text node is created. CDATA sections in documents are represented as text nodes as well where the parent element is the element in which the CDATA section is defined. If the element containing the CDATA section is the root element, the root element will have a text node. If any element already has a text node, the contents of the CDATA section are added to the existing contents of the text node. This ensures that the text node contains the entire textual contents of the related element. Because references and CDATA sections are resolved before the text node is created, there's no way to determine that the text originally contained references or CDATA sections.

- **Comment** Represents comments inserted into XML documents. All comments inserted into a document become comment nodes (except for comments in a DTD or schema). The text of the comment is everything inside the comment except for the opening <!-- and closing -->, respectively.
- **Processing instruction** Represents processing instructions in XML documents. Processing instruction nodes contain two values: the name of the instruction, which can be obtained with the name() function, and a string containing the rest of the processing instruction, but not including the opening <? or closing ?>, respectively.
- **Namespace** Represents namespaces declared in XSLT stylesheets. Namespace nodes are used by the XSLT processor and aren't meant to be used by stylesheet developers. Namespace nodes contain the value assigned to an element's xmlns attribute. The xmlns attribute isn't represented as an attribute node.

Each of these node types has a built-in template rule associated with it that allows the node to be processed as necessary. The following sections examine these built-in template rules.

Understanding the Element and Root Nodes Template

The built-in template for element and root nodes is used to process the root node and all of its child nodes. The template is defined as:

```
<xsl:template match="*|/">
   <xsl:apply-templates/>
</xsl:template>
```

As shown, the template match value is defined as:

```
*|/
```

These characters represent an XPath expression and all have special meaning:

- * is a wildcard character, indicating that any value is allowed. In the match attribute, this says match any element name.
- | is a choice indicator, indicating to match either by using the asterisk (*) or the slash (/).
- / is the designator for the root node. XPath refers to the root node using this designator.

Thus, when you put these characters together, all element nodes and the root node are deemed matches for the XPath expression. The xsl:apply-templates statement tells the XSLT processor to apply the appropriate templates to nodes in the input document. This ensures that any node in the document can be processed, even if there are no template rules for parent nodes.

Understanding the Modes Template

The xsl:template element has a mode attribute that lets you process the same set of nodes using different template rules. The built-in template that ensures modes are recognized is:

```
<xsl:template match="*|/" mode="x">
    <xsl:apply-templates mode="x"/>
</xsl:template>
```

This template ensures that element and root nodes are processed regardless of the mode that's currently being used. The mode template is only invoked when you define modes in your XSLT stylesheet, and then the template only works to ensure that the various modes are recognized.

Understanding the Text and Attribute Nodes Template

The built-in template for text and attribute nodes ensures that these nodes can be processed regardless of their value. This template is defined as:

```
<xsl:template match="text()|@*">
    <xsl:value-of select="."/>
</xsl:template>
```

As shown, the template match value is defined as:

```
text()|@*
```

These characters represent an XPath expression:

- text() is a reference to a function. The text() function is used to obtain the text contents of an element.
- | is a choice indicator, indicating to match either by using the text() function or the @* expression.
- @* is an expression that obtains the value of attributes.

Thus, the expression says to obtain the contents of any text or attribute node. The value-of select="." statement tells the XSLT processor to select these contents and copy them to the output tree. This template is only invoked when you define a template rule that attempts to access the contents of a text or attribute node, and in this case only the contents of the specified node are copied to the node tree.

Understanding Other Built-In Templates

The built-in template for comments and processing instructions is defined as:

```
<xsl:template match="comment()|processing-
instruction()" />
```

This is similar to the built-in template for namespaces, which is defined as:

```
<xsl:template match="namespace()" />
```

These built-in templates define no rules for comment, processing-instruction, and namespace nodes. Essentially, this is the same as saying don't do anything. These templates are only invoked when you define template rules that access comment, processing-instruction, or namespace nodes, and then the templates only work to ensure that the nodes are recognized. If you want the contents of these nodes to be extracted, you must define specific template rules to handle this.

12. Structuring XSLT Stylesheets

XSLT stylesheets are used to transform XML documents into another format. To do this, stylesheets contain rules that match various parts of the input document to a template that specifies how to format that particular part of the document. Every XSLT stylesheet is itself an XML document that contains three basic structures:

- An XSLT declaration that marks the start of the stylesheet.
- An output declaration that sets the output format.
- Template rules containing declarations.

Typically, these structures are applied in the order specified. This means that you start the stylesheet with the XSLT declaration, insert an optional output declaration, and then define template rules containing declarations.

Because an XSLT stylesheet is an XML document, it can start with a standard XML declaration that specifies the XML version, such as:

```
<?xml version="1.0"?>
```

However, the XML declaration isn't required and is omitted in most cases.

The optional XML declaration is followed by the <stylesheet> element, which defines the XSLT version being used and defines the namespace for XSLT definitions. The standard stylesheet declaration for XSLT version 2.0 is:

```
<xsl:stylesheet version="2.0"
  xmlns:xsl="http://www.w3.org/1999/XSL/Transform">
```

This declaration sets the namespace prefix as xsl and points to the Uniform Resource Identifier (URI) *http://www.w3.org/1999/XSL/Transform/*. Different versions of XSLT use a different namespace URI and version number. The closing tag for the stylesheet element is </stylesheet>. This means the basic form of a stylesheet is:

```
<xsl:stylesheet version="2.0"
  xmlns:xsl="http://www.w3.org/1999/XSL/Transform">
...
</xsl:stylesheet>
```

For ease of reference, XSLT stylesheets normally are saved with the .xsl extension. The .xsl extension ensures that the document is easily recognized as containing XSL and that applications, such as Microsoft Internet Explorer, view the document as such.

To define an XSLT stylesheet, follow these steps:

1. Type **<xsl:stylesheet** to declare the namespace prefix as xsl.

2. Specify the XSLT version number using **version="1.0"**, **version="1.1"**, **version="2.0"** or **version="3.0"**.

3. Specify the namespace for the stylesheet by typing **xmlns:xsl="http://www.w3.org/1999/XSL/Transform**.

4. Close the tag by typing **>**.

5. Type a few blank lines where you'll later enter the body of the stylesheet.

6. Type **</xsl:stylesheet>** to complete the stylesheet.

The result should look similar to the following:

```
<xsl:stylesheet version="2.0"
  xmlns:xsl="http://www.w3.org/1999/XSL/Transform">
...
</xsl:stylesheet>
```

You also could add the namespace for XSL-FO:

```
xmlns:fo="http://www.w3.org/1999/XSL/Format"
```

The result would then look similar to the following:

```
<xsl:stylesheet version="2.0"
  xmlns:xsl="http://www.w3.org/1999/XSL/Transform"
  xmlns:fo="http://www.w3.org/1999/XSL/Format">
...
</xsl:stylesheet>
```

13. Defining the Output Format

You specify the format for output documents using the `output` element. Although this element has no required attributes, it has many optional attributes. These attributes and their uses are discussed in the following sections.

Setting Attributes for the output Element

The primary attribute of the `output` element that you'll use is method, which sets the output method. The XSLT specification defines three possible output methods that processors are required to support:

- **method="xml"** Used when the output contains XML or an XML-based application, such as content formatted with XML-FO or content that uses Scalable Vector Graphics (SVG).
- **method="html"** Used when the output contains standard HTML.
- **method="text"** Used when the output contains text characters. These characters could represent standard text or the source code for a programming language.

> **Note** Because XHTML is an XML-based application, you could set the output method to method="xml" when you want the output document to be formatted as XHTML. You could also set method="html". If you do this, be sure to set attributes that build the appropriate XML and DOCTYPE declarations. For an example, see the section of this chapter entitled "Formatting Output as XML or XML-Based Markup."

The default output method is either XML or HTML, as determined by the contents of the `output`. If the `output` contains text and the root element is named `html` (in any combination of uppercase or lowercase characters), the default output method is HTML. Otherwise, the default output method is XML.

Although XSLT processors are free to implement other output methods, these are the standard output methods. The following example shows how you could set the output method to text:

```
<xsl:stylesheet version="2.0"
  xmlns:xsl="http://www.w3.org/1999/XSL/Transform">

<xsl:output method="text" />
...
</xsl:stylesheet>
```

Table 13-1 provides a summary of the `output` element's attributes. Example procedures using essential attributes with each of the standard output types are discussed in the following sections.

Table 13-1. Attributes of the XSLT output Element

Attribute	Description
cdata-section-elements	Lists elements that should be written as CDATA sections in the output. Processor will escape characters as necessary to ensure contents can be output. Used with method="xml".
doctype-public	Sets the public identifier to be used in the document type declaration. Used with method="xml" or method="html".
doctype-system	Sets the system identifier to be used in the document type declaration. Used with method="xml" or method="html".
encoding	Defines the character encoding to set in the XML or HTML declaration or the preferred encoding for

	text. Used with method="xml", method="html" or method="text".
indent	Determines whether the processor can indent the tags in the output document. The value must be yes or no. Processors aren't required to indent. Used with method="xml" or method="html"
media-type	Sets the media type (Multipurpose Internet Mail Extension [MIME] content type) of the output data. Used with method="xml", method="html" or method="text".
method	Sets the output method. Typically, the value is xml, html, or text.
omit-xml-declaration	Determines whether the processor should omit the XML declaration in the output. The value must be yes or no. Used with method="xml".
standalone	Sets the standalone attribute in the XML declaration of the output document. The value must be yes or no. Used with method="xml".
version	Sets the version attribute of the HTML or XML declaration in the output document. Used with method="xml" or method="html".

Formatting Output as XML or XML-Based Markup

XML is one of the two default output formats for XSLT stylesheets. Output is formatted as XML any time the output doesn't contain a root element named html (in any combination of upper or lowercase characters). If you like, you can explicitly specify that the output should be formatted as XML. Simply set method="xml" in the output element of the stylesheet, as shown in this example:

```
<xsl:stylesheet version="2.0"
```

```
xmlns:xsl="http://www.w3.org/1999/XSL/Transform">

<xsl:output method="xml" />
…
</xsl:stylesheet>
```

When you define the output as XML, you can set attributes that build the output document's XML declaration. The key attributes are: version, standalone, and encoding—version sets the XML version being used; standalone specifies whether the document is a stand-alone document that doesn't use external files; encoding specifies the character encoding of the output document. If you don't specify values for these attributes, the XML declaration is created as:

```
<?xml version="1.0" encoding="UTF-8"?>
```

and the document is considered to be a standalone document (using the assumed default, as discussed in the section of Chapter 7 entitled "Using the Standalone Attribute"). You can modify the default values by setting explicit values. For example, if you wanted the XML declaration to look like this:

```
<?xml version="1.0" encoding="ISO-8859_1"
standalone="yes"?>
```

you'd set the attributes of the output element like this:

```
<xsl:output method="xml" version="1.0"
encoding="ISO-8859_1" standalone="yes"/>
```

Any time the output is formatted using an application of XML, such as XML-FO or Scalable Vector Graphics (SVG), you should explicitly set the output method as XML and then define any additional attributes necessary to properly interpret the output document. With SVG, for example, you'll want to set the public and system identifiers so that a DOCTYPE declaration containing these values will be created in the output document. To do this, you set the doctype-public and doctype-system attributes of the output element. With SVG, the standard values for these attributes are "-//W3C//DTD SVG 1.1//EN"

and "http://www.w3.org/Graphics/SVG/1.1/DTD/svg11.dtd",
respectively.

> **Note** The value EN in the PUBLIC URI for SVG is the two-letter language code for U.S. English. If the document isn't formatted in U.S. English, you must change the language code to the appropriate value.

The following example shows how you could set the doctype-public and doctype-system attributes in a stylesheet:

```
<?xml version="1.0"?>
<xsl:stylesheet version="3.0"
xmlns:xsl="http://www.w3.org/1999/XSL/Transform">

   <xsl:output method="xml"
     doctype-public="-//W3C//DTD SVG 1.1//EN"
     doctype-system=
"http://www.w3.org/Graphics/SVG/1.1/DTD/svg11.dtd"/>

  <xsl:template match="/">
   <svg>
   ...
   </svg>
  </xsl:template>

</xsl:stylesheet>
```

In the output document these values would be defined like this:

```
<?xml version="1.0" encoding="UTF-8"?>
<!DOCTYPE svg PUBLIC "-//W3C//DTD SVG 1.1//EN"
"http://www.w3.org/Graphics/SVG/1.1/DTD/svg11.dtd">
<svg>
...
</svg>
```

You can also use the `doctype-public` and `doctype-system` attributes when you want to format output as XHTML. With XHTML, these attributes are set to "-//W3C//DTD XHTML 2.0 Strict//EN" and "http://www.w3.org/TR/xhtml2/DTD/xhtml2-strict.dtd", respectively in most cases. This means a typical stylesheet for XHTML looks like this:

```
<?xml version="1.0"?>
<xsl:stylesheet version="3.0"
xmlns:xsl="http://www.w3.org/1999/XSL/Transform">

  <xsl:output method="xml"
    doctype-public="-//W3C//DTD XHTML 2.0 Strict//EN"
    doctype-system=
"http://www.w3.org/TR/xhtml2/DTD/xhtml2-strict.dtd"/>

  <xsl:template match="/">
   <html>
   ...
   </html>
  </xsl:template>

</xsl:stylesheet>
```

and these values appear in the output document like this:

```
<?xml version="1.0" encoding="UTF-8"?>
<!DOCTYPE xhtml PUBLIC "-//W3C//DTD XHTML 2.0 Strict//EN"
"http://www.w3.org/TR/xhtml2/DTD/xhtml2-strict.dtd ">
<html>
...
</html>
```

> **Note** As before, the value EN in the PUBLIC URI is the two-letter language code for U.S. English. If the document isn't formatted in U.S. English, you must change the language code to the appropriate value. The PUBLIC and SYSTEM URIs also reference the strict version of the XHTML 2.0 DTD. References to transitional and frameset are also possible.

Now that you've seen basic examples, lets take a more detailed look at the conversion process. The following example defines an XSLT stylesheet that formats the example XML document used earlier in the text using XML-FO:

```xml
<?xml version="1.0"?>
<xsl:stylesheet version="3.0"
xmlns:xsl="http://www.w3.org/1999/XSL/Transform"
xmlns:fo="http://www.w3.org/1999/XSL/Format">

 <xsl:output method="xml"/>

 <xsl:template match="/">
  <fo:root
xmlns:fo="http://www.w3.org/1999/XSL/Format">
   <fo:layout-master-set>
    <fo:simple-page-master margin-right="50pt"
margin-left="50pt"
     page-height="11in" page-width="8.5in"
     margin-bottom="35pt" margin-top="35pt" master-
name="main">
     <fo:region-before extent="25pt"/>
     <fo:region-body margin-top="50pt" margin-
bottom="50pt"/>
     <fo:region-after extent="25pt"/>
    </fo:simple-page-master>
    <fo:page-sequence-master master-name="standard">
     <fo:repeatable-page-master-alternatives>
      <fo:conditional-page-master-reference
          master-name="main" odd-or-even="any"/>
     </fo:repeatable-page-master-alternatives>
    </fo:page-sequence-master>
   </fo:layout-master-set>

   <fo:page-sequence master-name="standard">
    <fo:flow flow-name="xsl-region-body">
     <xsl:apply-templates select="document"/>
    </fo:flow>
   </fo:page-sequence>
  </fo:root>
 </xsl:template>

 <xsl:template match="document">
```

```
 <fo:block line-height="16pt" font-size="12pt"
text-align="left">
   <xsl:value-of select="."/>
  </fo:block>
 </xsl:template>

</xsl:stylesheet>
```

Here, the stylesheet applies formatting to the document using XML-FO. The formatting entries set the page size to 8 ½" x 11"; define a master page layout with margins for the top, bottom, left, and right sides of the page; and then define the formatting for the body of the page. Using an XSLT processor, we could use this stylesheet to transform the sample.xml document defined previously.

The output of the transformation process is the following XML document containing formatted objects:

```
<?xml version="1.0" encoding="UTF-8"?>
<fo:root
xmlns:fo="http://www.w3.org/1999/XSL/Format">
 <fo:layout-master-set>
  <fo:simple-page-master margin-right="50pt" margin-
left="50pt"
   page-height="11in" page-width="8.5in"
   margin-bottom="35pt" margin-top="35pt" master-
name="main">
    <fo:region-before extent="25pt"/>
    <fo:region-body margin-top="50pt" margin-
bottom="50pt"/>
    <fo:region-after extent="25pt"/>
  </fo:simple-page-master>
  <fo:page-sequence-master master-name="standard">
   <fo:repeatable-page-master-alternatives>
    <fo:conditional-page-master-reference
        master-name="main" odd-or-even="any"/>
   </fo:repeatable-page-master-alternatives>
  </fo:page-sequence-master>
 </fo:layout-master-set>

 <fo:page-sequence master-name="standard">
  <fo:flow flow-name="xsl-region-body">
```

```
    <fo:block line-height="16pt" font-size="12pt"
text-align="left">
    XSLT is a powerful transformation language.
    </fo:block>
  </fo:flow>
 </fo:page-sequence>
</fo:root>
```

You can easily convert documents that use XML-FO to other document formats, such as Adobe's PDF. Once you convert the document to PDF, you could view it in Adobe Acrobat.

> **Real World** I hope you're starting to see the true power of XSLT as a document transformation powerhouse. Imagine implementing automated transformations for an e-commerce Web site. Here, you could extract data formatted as XML directly from a database and then use XSLT to transform the data into a document in any desired output format.

Formatting Output as HTML

HTML is the other default output format for XSLT stylesheets. Output is formatted as HTML any time the output contains text and has a root element named html (in any combination of upper or lowercase characters). If you like, you can explicitly specify that the output should be formatted as HTML. Simply set method="html" in the stylesheet, as shown in this example:

```
<xsl:stylesheet version="2.0"
  xmlns:xsl="http://www.w3.org/1999/XSL/Transform">

  <xsl:output method="html"/>

  <xsl:template match="/">
    <xsl:apply-templates select="document"/>
  </xsl:template>
```

```
<xsl:template match="document">
  <html>
    <body>
      <p>
        <xsl:value-of select="."/>
      </p>
    </body>
  </html>
</xsl:template>

</xsl:stylesheet>
```

You saw this example earlier in the text used to convert the sample XML document to HTML. Because XSLT is so versatile, there are always additional ways to perform tasks. To create the same output document, you could have also used the following XSLT template:

```
<xsl:stylesheet version="2.0"
  xmlns:xsl="http://www.w3.org/1999/XSL/Transform">

  <xsl:output method="html"/>

  <xsl:template match="/">
    <html>
      <body>
        <xsl:apply-templates select="document"/>
      </body>
    </html>
  </xsl:template>

  <xsl:template match="document">
      <p>
        <xsl:value-of select="."/>
      </p>
  </xsl:template>

</xsl:stylesheet>
```

The subtle difference between this template and the previous template is that the html and body elements are built in the root template and only the contents of the document element are evaluated in the second template. This subtle change lets you easily handle the case where there are multiple document elements and you want to output a properly formatted document. For example, if you rewrote the sample document to contain multiple document elements like this:

```
<?xml version="1.0"?>
<definitions>
 <document>
  XML is a language for describing other languages.
 </document>
 <document>
  XSLT is a powerful transformation language.
 </document>
</definitions>
```

the modified stylesheet would ensure that the output document was formatted like this:

```
<html>
<body>
<p>
  XML is a language for describing other languages.
</p>
<p>
  XSLT is a powerful transformation language.
</p>
</body>
</html>
```

Without this change, we'd end up with a document that was incorrectly formatted and looked like this:

```
<html>
<body>
<p>
  XML is a language for describing other languages.
</p>
</body>
</html>
<html>
<body>
```

```
<p>
   XSLT is a powerful transformation language.
</p>
</body>
</html>
```

When you use HTML, you'll often want to associate the output with a cascading style sheet or make direct style assignments. If you've worked with HTML and CSS before, defining style for an output document formatted as HTML is easy. Consider the following example output document that has two styles for paragraph tags defined:

```
<html>
   <head>
   <title>Using Classes in Style Sheets</title>
   <style type="text/css">
     <!--
     p.styleA  {font: 45pt Times; color: brown}
     p.styleB  {font: 30pt Arial; color: blue}
     -->
   </style>
   </head>
   <body>
      <p class="styleA"> This is a paragraph in
styleA</p>
      <p class="styleB"> This is a paragraph in
styleB</p>
   <body>
</html>
```

To transform an XML document into an HTML that looks like this, you'd define the XSLT stylesheet like this:

```
<xsl:stylesheet version="2.0"
   xmlns:xsl="http://www.w3.org/1999/XSL/Transform">

   <xsl:output method="html"/>

   <xsl:template match="/">
     <html>
       <head>
```

```
        <title>Using Classes in Style Sheets</title>
        <style type="text/css">
          <xsl:comment>
          p.styleA   {font: 45pt Times; color:
brown}

          p.styleB   {font: 30pt Arial; color: blue}
          </xsl:comment>
        </style>
      </head>
      <body>
          <xsl:apply-templates
select="definitions/document1"/>
          <xsl:apply-templates
select="definitions/document2"/>
      </body>
    </html>
  </xsl:template>

  <xsl:template match="document1">
        <p class="styleA">
          <xsl:value-of select="."/>
        </p>
  </xsl:template>

  <xsl:template match="document2">
        <p class="styleB">
          <xsl:value-of select="."/>
        </p>
  </xsl:template>

</xsl:stylesheet>
```

In this example, note that the HTML comment tags (<!-- and -->) are
replaced with the xsl:comment tags (<xsl:comment> and
</xsl:comment>) and that template matches are for elements named
document1 and document2, respectively. document1 and
document2 are arbitrary names that represent elements in the input
document that you want to format with either styleA or styleB. You
could replace these arbitrary names with the names of any valid
elements from the input document.

Although you can make internal style assignments, cascading style sheets are more typically defined externally. In HTML, you specify the location of an external cascading style sheet using the link element in the form:

```
<link rel="stylesheet" type="text/css"
href="mystyles.css">
```

In the XSLT stylesheet that defines your output HTML document, you could insert this link element directly with one noteworthy exception. You'd have to define the linked stylesheet as an empty element, such as:

```
<link rel="stylesheet" type="text/css"
href="mystyles.css" />
```

You could then insert the link element directly into the XSLT stylesheet as shown in this example:

```
<xsl:stylesheet version="2.0"
  xmlns:xsl="http://www.w3.org/1999/XSL/Transform">

  <xsl:output method="html"/>

  <xsl:template match="/">
    <html>
      <head>
        <link rel="stylesheet" type="text/css"
href="mystyles.css" />
      </head>
      <body>
        <xsl:apply-templates select="document"/>
      </body>
    </html>
  </xsl:template>

  <xsl:template match="document">
      <p>
        <xsl:value-of select="."/>
      </p>
  </xsl:template>
```

```
</xsl:stylesheet>
```

Formatting Output as Text or Program Source Code

Whenever you want to format the output document as text or program source code, you specify the output format as method="text". Afterward, you insert the literal text or source code into `xsl:text` elements. Here's a basic example of an XSLT stylesheet that's used to output text:

```
<xsl:stylesheet version="2.0"
  xmlns:xsl="http://www.w3.org/1999/XSL/Transform">

  <xsl:output method="html"/>

  <xsl:template match="/">
    <xsl:apply-templates select="document"/>
  </xsl:template>

  <xsl:template match="document">
    <xsl:text>
The contents of the document element are:
    </xsl:text>
    <xsl:value-of select="."/>
    <xsl:text>

.

    </xsl:text>
  </xsl:template>

</xsl:stylesheet>
```

If the input XML document for this stylesheet looked like this:

```
<?xml version="1.0"?>
<document>
XSLT, XML, XSL-FO
</document>
```

the output after transformation would look like this:

```
The contents of the document element are: XSLT, XML,
XSL-FO.
```

With source code, the trick is to ensure that you apply templates and switch to literal text in the appropriate locations to get the exact output you desire. Consider the following Java source:

```
class hello {
  public static void main(String[] args) {
    System.out.println("Hello, " + args[0] + "!");
  }
}
```

This short snippet of code writes a string to the standard output. If the program is run with the command:

```
java Hello William
```

the output string is:

```
Hello, William!
```

You could rewrite this program within an XSLT stylesheet so that the program gets its output argument from the contents of a specific element. For example, if your XML document was defined as:

```
<?xml version="1.0"?>
<name>
Bob
</name>
```

an XSLT stylesheet that used the document with the previous Java source code would look like this:

```
<?xml version="1.0"?>
<xsl:stylesheet version="3.0"
  xmlns:xsl="http://www.w3.org/1999/XSL/Transform">

  <xsl:output method="text"/>

  <xsl:template match="/">
    <xsl:text>
      class hello {
```

```
          public static void main(String[] args) {
   </xsl:text>
   <xsl:apply-templates select="name"/>
   <xsl:text>
          }
       }
   </xsl:text>
</xsl:template>

<xsl:template match="name">
   <xsl:text>System.out.println("Hello, </xsl:text>
   <xsl:value-of select="."/>
   <xsl:text>!");</xsl:text>
</xsl:template>

</xsl:stylesheet>
```

Based on the contents of the input document, the output after transformation is:

```
class hello {
  public static void main(String[] args) {
    System.out.println("Hello, Bob!");
  }
}
```

> **Note** More precisely, the output would contain a few extra spaces because of how the name tag is defined and used in the template. To get rid of these extra spaces, you could replace value of select="." with value of select="normalize-space()".

Setting the Output Format

As you've seen, you can transform XML documents in many ways using XSLT. Regardless of which output format you choose, the basic steps you follow to set the output format are the same. These steps are:

1. After the begin stylesheet element, type **<xsl:output**.

2. If you want to set a specific output method other than the default, type **method="*format*"**, where *format* sets the output format. The standard values are xml, html, and text.

3. Specify other attributes for the output element as necessary. For example, if you wanted to encode the document using ISO 8859 Latin 1, you'd set **encoding="ISO-8859_1"**.

4. Type **/>** to complete the output element.

The result should look similar to the following:

```
<xsl:output method="format" attrib1="value"
attrib2="value" attribN="value"/>
```

14. Defining Template Rules and Declarations

The processes of defining template rules and making template declarations go hand in hand. Whenever you define a template rule, you use a set of matching criteria to determine which template should be processed. The contents of the template rule are the individual declarations that you want to make. (Throughout this text, I refer to the template rule and the declarations it contains as a template).

The following sections examine basic techniques you can use to define template rules and declarations.

Creating the Root Template

As previously explained in this text, all templates are processed recursively, starting with the root template. This means that the root template is at the top of the execution tree and all other templates are processed after the root template. The basic format of a template rule that matches the root node is:

```
<xsl:template match="/">
...
</xsl:template>
```

Although you can enter templates in any order in the XSLT stylesheet, you'll usually want the root template to be at the top of the stylesheet and other templates to follow. With this in mind, the steps you follow to create the root template are

1. After you've defined the stylesheet's start tag and output method, type **<xsl:template**.

2. Type **match="/">** to indicate that the template rule should match the root node and complete the xsl:template element.

3. Create template rules for other nodes in the input document as specified in the next section of this chapter (which is titled "Creating and Applying Template Rules.")

4. Type **</xsl:template>** to complete the template.

Your stylesheet should now look similar to this:

```
<xsl:stylesheet version="2.0"
  xmlns:xsl="http://www.w3.org/1999/XSL/Transform">

  <xsl:output method="html"/>

  <xsl:template match="/">
  ...
  </xsl:template>

</xsl:stylesheet>
```

Creating and Applying Template Rules

Template rules describe how a particular section of a document should be output. The basic format of a template rule is:

```
<xsl:template match="pattern">
...
</xsl:template>
```

where *pattern* identifies the sections of the document to which the template should be applied. The inner section of the template rule determines what happens when a match is found. To ensure that another template rule is processed, you must use the `apply-templates` element to select the node or nodes that you want to process. The basic format of the `apply-templates` element is:

```
<xsl:apply-templates select="expression"/>
```

where *expression* is an XPath expression that identifies the nodes whose templates should be applied.

To perform some other type of processing, you must specify the appropriate actions. For example, to display the value of nodes that match the template rule, you could use the xsl:value-of element as discussed in the next section of this chapter, entitled "Outputting the Contents of Nodes."

Template rules are recursively processed starting with the template rule for the root node. To take advantage of recursion, you typically apply templates for top-level nodes in the root template, the next level nodes inside the templates for top-level nodes, and so on. For example, if the input document looked like this:

```
<?xml version="1.0"?>
<root>
  <elementA id="s1">
   <elementB>B1's contents
   </elementB>
   <elementC>C1's contents
   </elementC>
   <elementD>D1's contents
   </elementD>
  <elementA>

  <elementA id="s2">
   <elementB>B2's contents
   </elementB>
   <elementC>C2's contents
   </elementC>
   <elementD>D2's contents
   </elementD>
  <elementA>
</root>
```

you might define the set of template rules that processes these elements as:

```
<xsl:template match="/">
  <xsl:apply-templates select="elementA"/>
</xsl:template>

<xsl:template match="elementA">
  <xsl:apply-templates select="elementB"/>
  <xsl:apply-templates select="elementC"/>
  <xsl:apply-templates select="elementD"/>
</xsl:template>

<xsl:template match="elementB">
...
</xsl:template>

<xsl:template match="elementC">
...
</xsl:template>

<xsl:template match="elementD">
...
</xsl:template>
```

This would ensure that nodes are processed recursively in the following order:

root → elementA id="s1" → elementB1 → elementC1 →

elementD1 → elementA id="s2" → elementB2 →

elementC2 → elementD2

To create a template rule that applies another template, follow these steps:

1. After you've defined the stylesheet's start tag and output method, type **<xsl:template match="*pattern*">**, where *pattern* identifies the sections of the document to which the template should be applied.

2. Type **<xsl:apply-templates select="*expression*"/>**, where *expression* identifies the nodes whose templates should be applied. Repeat this step to apply other template rules.

3. Type **</xsl:template>** to complete the template.

The result should look similar to the following:

```
<xsl:template match="pattern">
  <xsl:apply-templates select="expression1"/>
  <xsl:apply-templates select="expression2"/>
  ...
  <xsl:apply-templates select="expressionN"/>
</xsl:template>
```

Outputting the Contents of Nodes

After you define template rules for the root element and top-level elements, you'll want to define rules that apply to low-level elements that contain text. In most cases you'll want to display the value of this text in the output document. As shown in previous examples, you can use the `xsl:value-of` element to display the contents of a particular node. The basic format of this element is:

```
<xsl:value-of select="expression" />
```

where *expression* identifies the node or nodes whose content should be output at the current position in the output document.

In most of the previous expression examples, I've used the value . to specify that the contents of the current node should be displayed. Although you can reference the current node, you can reference any other node in the document as well. For example, you can reference the child node of the current node simply by entering the name of the child node. These values are XPath expressions called location paths, which you'll learn about in Chapters 15 - 17.

Following this discussion, you could output the contents of the current node or a child node of the current node by following these steps:

1. Within the template rule that you want to work with, type **<xsl:value-of** to begin the declaration.

2. Type **select="."/>** to specify the current node's contents or type **select="*name*"/>** to specify that the contents of the named child element of the current element should be output.

The result should be similar to the following.

```
<xsl:template match="pattern">
  <xsl:value-of select="." />
</xsl:template>
```

15. XPath Operators & Expressions

XSL Transformations (XSLT) uses XML Path (XPath) to access and refer to parts of an input document. XPath locates various document structures by representing those structures as node trees that can be navigated using location paths. The location paths have a very specific syntax that includes operators and expressions used to locate parts of a document according to the type of structure they represent. The basic structures that location paths allow you to access include

- **Root nodes** Represent the root element in XML documents
- **Element nodes** Represent all elements in XML documents, including root nodes
- **Attribute nodes** Represent attributes in XML documents, including default and inherited attributes (but excluding xmlns attributes)
- **Text nodes** Represent the text contents of elements including any CDATA sections that elements might contain
- **Comment nodes** Represent the text components of comments that are inserted into XML documents
- **Processing instruction nodes** Represent processing instructions in XML documents by name and string value
- **Namespace nodes** Represent namespaces declared in XSLT stylesheets as defined in xmlns attributes

As you learned in previous chapters, you can refer to these node types as part of match and select expressions for various XSLT elements. This allows you to create template rules that match various node types and then to specify the transformations that should be applied to those node types. The catch is that the only part of an XSLT stylesheet that's processed automatically is the template rule for a root node, which is referred to by the location path /. Because of this, you use template rules for root nodes to start the transformation process and typically design your XSLT stylesheets to use recursion to extract information from input documents.

Recursion is a powerful aspect of XSLT. It allows you to locate various structures according to their context in a document. Essentially, you work from the root context in a document to the top-level nodes and then you explore successive levels of nodes associated with each top-level node until you've examined all the structures in a document that you want to work with.

The / representing the root node is only one of the many XPath expressions you can use. Each expression follows a specific syntax and can make use of various operators to locate specific types of nodes. You can access nodes using location paths that are context-specific as well as by using paths that are context-free.

The basic difference between context-specific and context-free location paths has to do with which nodes are located. With context-specific location paths, nodes are evaluated according to the context in which they appear, allowing you to match a node relative to its location in a document. With context-free location paths, nodes are evaluated directly and outside of a specific context, allowing you to locate nodes by specifying their absolute location without regard to the current context. To better understand the impact of context, consider the following XML document:

```
<?xml version="1.0" ?>
<inventory>
    <item tracking_number="459323" manufacturer="Not
listed">
        <item_type>Fiberglass Prehung Entry
Door</item_type>
        <description>6-panel left-hand inswing entry
door, primed, white</description>
    </item>
    <item tracking_number="459789" manufacturer="Not
listed">
```

```
    <item_type>Steel Prehung Entry
Door</item_type>
    <description>4-panel left-hand inswing entry
door, primed, black, steel</description>
  </item>
</inventory>
```

A basic node tree representing the elements of this document could look like this:

```
-inventory
  -item
    -item_type
    -description
  -item
    -item_type
    -description
```

Essentially, this node tree representation says that the root element, inventory, has two item elements as its only children. The item elements in turn have two child elements called item_type and description.

You could locate these elements using many techniques. The following example uses recursion to work with elements in a context-specific manner:

```
<xsl:template match="/">
    <html>
      <body>
       <xsl:apply-templates
select="inventory/item"/>
      </body>
    </html>
</xsl:template>

<xsl:template match="item">
  <xsl:apply-templates select="item_type"/>
  <xsl:apply-templates select="description"/>
</xsl:template>

<xsl:template match="item_type">
<h1>
```

```
<xsl:value-of select="."/>
</h1>
</xsl:template>

<xsl:template match="description">
<p>
<xsl:value-of select="."/>
</p>
</xsl:template>
```

Real World Namespaces are tracked separately by XSLT processors using namespace nodes. Every root, element, and attribute node defined in a document can have a namespace associated with it. If so, you must reference the qualified name in your XSLT stylesheets. For example, if the namespace for the inventory document were inv, you'd reference `inv:item`, `inv:item_type`, and `inv:description` rather than `item`, `item_type`, and `description`, respectively.

Based on this XSLT stylesheet, the inventory document is processed in the following order:

root → item1 → item_type → description → item2 → item_type → description

and the output document would look like this:

```
<html>
<body>
<h1>Fiberglass Prehung Entry Door</h1>
<p>6-panel left-hand inswing entry door, primed,
white</p>
<h1>Steel Prehung Entry Door</h1>
<p>4-panel left-hand inswing entry door, primed,
black, steel</p>
</body>
```

```
</html>
```

When you work with the current context, XPath expressions are evaluated relative to the context node. Because expressions can match multiple nodes, the XSLT processor maintains a pointer of sorts that tracks the context position and the context size. The context position refers to the position of the node currently being processed. The context size refers to the number of nodes selected by the current expression. Together, the context position and context size allow the XSLT processor to navigate the node tree in terms of the current context.

If the inventory document contained a single item element whose contents we wanted to work with directly, such as:

```
<?xml version="1.0" ?>
<inventory>
    <summary>Inventory Summary for 12 - 15 -
16</summary>
    <item tracking_number="459323" manufacturer="Not
listed">
        <item_type>Fiberglass Prehung Entry
Door</item_type>
        <description>6-panel left-hand inswing entry
door, primed, white</description>
    </item>
    <details>No details available.</details>
</inventory>
```

we could process the item element directly rather than in terms of the current context. Here's an example:

```
<xsl:template match="/">
    <html>
      <body>
        <h1>
          <xsl:apply-templates
select="/inventory/item/item_type"/>
        </h1>

        <p>
```

```
            <xsl:apply-templates
select="/inventory/item/description"/>
           </p>

        </body>
      </html>
</xsl:template>
```

In this example you specify the elements you want to work with using an absolute path. Absolute paths differ from relative paths in that they're always located in terms of the root element rather than in terms of the current context. The first apply-templates declaration:

```
<xsl:apply-templates
select="/inventory/item/item_type"/>
```

specifies that there's a root element called inventory that contains an item element that in turn has an item_type element associated with it. This expression tells the XSLT processor to return all nodes that have this absolute path. In the previous document, this would mean that the processor would return the node defined as follows:

```
<item_type>Fiberglass Prehung Entry Door</item_type>
```

The second apply-templates declaration:

```
<xsl:apply-templates
select="/inventory/item/description"/>
```

specifies that there's a root element called inventory that contains an item element that in turn has a description element associated with it. This expression tells the XSLT processor to return all nodes that have this absolute path. In the previous document, this would mean that the processor would return the node defined as follows:

```
<description>6-panel left-hand inswing entry door,
primed, white</description>
```

Based on this, the resulting output document would look like this:

```
<html>
<body>
<h1>Fiberglass Prehung Entry Door</h1>
<p>6-panel left-hand inswing entry door, primed,
white</p>
</body>
</html>
```

Unfortunately, these XSLT expressions wouldn't work the way you intended if the document contained multiple items subsets. Remember, the processor returns all matching nodes with the specified absolute path. To allow for the case where multiple items were in the inventory document and you wanted to use absolute paths, you'd have to modify the XSLT stylesheet. The following example shows one way you could do this:

```
<xsl:template match="/">
    <html>
      <body>
        <h1>Inventory Item Summary</h1>
        <xsl:apply-templates
select="/inventory/item/item_type"/>
        <h1>Description Summary</h1>
        <xsl:apply-templates
select="/inventory/item/description"/>
      </body>
    </html>
</xsl:template>

<xsl:template match="/inventory/item/item_type">
  <p>
    <xsl:value-of select="."/>
  </p>
</xsl:template>

<xsl:template match="/inventory/item/description">
  <p>
    <xsl:value-of select="."/>
  </p>
</xsl:template>
```

With the original inventory document defined as:

```
<?xml version="1.0" ?>
<inventory>
    <item tracking_number="459323" manufacturer="Not
listed">
        <item_type>Fiberglass Prehung Entry
Door</item_type>
        <description>6-panel left-hand inswing entry
door, primed, white</description>
    </item>
    <item tracking_number="459789" manufacturer="Not
listed">
        <item_type>Steel Prehung Entry
Door</item_type>
        <description>4-panel left-hand inswing entry
door, primed, black, steel</description>
    </item>
</inventory>
```

the output is now:

```
<html>
<body>
<h1>Inventory Item Summary</h1>
<p>Fiberglass Prehung Entry Door</p>
<p>Steel Prehung Entry Door</p>
<h1>Description Summary</h1>
<p>6-panel left-hand inswing entry door, primed,
white</p>
<p>4-panel left-hand inswing entry door, primed,
black, steel</p>
</body>
</html>
```

As you can see from the output, the item_type values are listed
first, followed by a list of description values. This output would be
useful if you wanted to list the contents of various elements in
separate lists. However, the output isn't optimal in this case. Here,
you might want to use relative paths and rework the XSLT stylesheet
accordingly.

16. Understanding XPath Operators and Datatypes

In previous chapters, you've seen various operators, such as . and /, used in examples. XPath defines many other operators that you can use in expressions to locate nodes. In this section I've divided these operators into three broad categories to provide a resource summary of the various operators that are available.

Table 16-1 summarizes standard XPath operators. These operators are the ones you'll use most often with XSLT and XPath.

Table 16-1. XPath Standard Operators

Operator	Description
/	A path separator used to indicate successive levels of the node tree hierarchy. If used at the beginning of an expression, it represents the root node.
.	Refers to the current context node.
..	Refers to the parent of the current context node.
@	Indicates an attribute reference.
*	A wildcard that selects any node of the principal node type; with element nodes, this would select or match any element node in the current context.

@*	A wildcard that selects or matches any attribute node in the current context.
node()	Selects all nodes in the current context regardless of type. (Technically, this is type of a node test that's used as a wildcard.)
//	Allows you to skip levels in the hierarchy; indicates that zero or more elements may occur between the slashes.
[]	Predicate operator used in predicate expressions to filter a group of nodes.
|	Selects either match in a series, such as match="a|b|c" to match a, b, and c elements.
$	Variable operator used to indicate variable names.

In addition to defining standard operators, XPath defines a set of mathematical and Boolean operators. These operators are summarized in Table 16-2. Although mathematical operators evaluate expressions to specific values, Boolean operators evaluate expressions as Booleans (either true or false). Booleans are only one of the several data types that can be used with XPath. Other datatypes include

- **node-set** Represents a set of nodes. Node sets can be empty or they can contain any number of nodes.
- **result tree fragment** A temporary tree that holds the value of a result or the value of variable assignment.

- **number** Represents a floating-point number. All floating-point numbers comply with IEEE 754 (which is the same standard used with float and double datatypes used by XML Schema). As with XML Schema, XPath and XSLT floating-point values have five special values: 0 (referred to as positive zero), -0 (referred to as negative zero), INF (referred to as positive infinity), -INF (referred to as negative infinity), and NaN (referred to as not-a-number).
- **string** Represents a sequence of zero or more characters as defined in the XML specification.

Table 16-2. XPath Arithmetic Operators

Operator	Description
*	Multiplication; multiplies one number by another.
div	Division; performs floating-point division on two numbers.
mod	Modulus; returns the floating-point remainder of dividing one number by another.
+	Addition; adds one number to another.
-	Subtraction; subtracts one number from another.
=	Equality; tests whether two expressions are equal.
<	Less than; tests whether the first expression is less than the second.
>	Greater than; tests whether the first expression is greater than the second.

<=	Less than or equals; tests whether the first expression is less than or equal to the second.
>=	Greater than or equals; tests whether the first expression is greater than or equal to the second.
!=	Not equal; tests whether the two expressions aren't equal.
and	Logical And; tests whether the first and the second expression are true. Both expressions must be true for the logical And to evaluate to true.
or	Logical Or; tests whether one of two expressions is true. Only one expression must be true for the logical Or to evaluate to true.

Another type of operator XPath defines is an axis. An axis is an operator keyword that acts as a location designator. You use axes to make unabbreviated XPath references. Axes are useful when you want to use advanced techniques to locate ancestor, descendent, and sibling nodes, but they're too complex for most other uses.

17. Using Relative XPath Expressions

Relative and absolute XPath expressions are similar to Uniform Resource Locators (URLs) used in hypertext references in the way they're used and structured. With relative XPath expressions, you reference locations relative to the current context that the XSLT processor is working with. Relative expressions refer to:

- The current context node using a single period (.)
- A parent of the current node using a double period (..)
- A child of the current node by referencing its name directly
- A named sibling of the current node by referencing ../name
- Nodes in other levels of the hierarchy by referencing their relative path from the current context

Techniques for working with these context-specific expressions are discussed in the following sections.

Referencing the Current Context Node

When you work with the current context, other XPath locations can be referenced relative to the current position. The XPath expression you use to reference the current node itself is a single period (.).

Essentially, the single period (.) says to use the current context node. In the following example, the contents of the current node are selected and output:

```
<xsl:template match="element">
  <html>
    <body>
```

```
      <p>
        <xsl:value-of select="."/>
      </p>
    </body>
  </html>
</xsl:template>
```

Following this, if you're currently processing the node that you want to use in a select statement, you can refer to the current node by completing these steps:

1. Type a single period, as in <xsl:value-of select="."/>.

2. Alternatively, specify a predicate expression that selects a subset of the current node, as discussed in the section of Chapter 21 entitled "Filtering To Match Nodes with Specific Values."

Referencing a Parent Node

You can reference the parent of the current context node using a double period (..), such as:

```
<xsl:value-of select=".."/>
```

Essentially, the double period (..) tells XPath to go up one level in the node tree hierarchy. For example, if the current context is processing the item_type elements based on this input document:

```
<?xml version="1.0" ?>
<inventory>
    <item tracking_number="459323" manufacturer="Not
listed">
        <item_type>Fiberglass Prehung Entry
Door</item_type>
        <description>6-panel left-hand inswing entry
door, primed, white</description>
    </item>
    <item tracking_number="459789" manufacturer="Not
listed">
```

```
    <item_type>Steel Prehung Entry
Door</item_type>
    <description>4-panel left-hand inswing entry
door, primed, black, steel</description>
  </item>
</inventory>
```

the parent elements referenced by .. are the item elements.

You can also reference the parent of a parent node. For example, if you were working with the description element and wanted to access the inventory element (which is the parent of the parent element item), you could extend the parent reference so that it went two levels up the tree using the value:

../..

> **Tip** This technique can be extended as far as necessary. If you need to go three levels up the node tree, you'd use ../../.., for four levels up the tree you'd use ../../../.., and so on.

You can select the parents of the current node by following these steps:

1. Type .. to select the parent of the current context node.

2. Optionally, type /.. to specify a parent of the parent node. Repeat this step to go farther up the hierarchy.

The result should look similar to the following:

```
<xsl:value-of select="../.."/>
```

Referencing Siblings Relative to the Current Context

Relative XPath expressions also allow you to locate nodes at the same level as the current context node. To do this, you reference the parent using double periods (..), enter a slash (/), and then specify the name of the sibling that you want to work with. For example, if you were working with the `item_type` element defined in the following inventory document:

```
<?xml version="1.0" ?>
<inventory>
    <item tracking_number="459323" manufacturer="Not
listed">
        <item_type>Fiberglass Prehung Entry
Door</item_type>
        <description>6-panel left-hand inswing entry
door, primed, white</description>
    </item>
    <item tracking_number="459789" manufacturer="Not
listed">
        <item_type>Steel Prehung Entry
Door</item_type>
        <description>4-panel left-hand inswing entry
door, primed, black, steel</description>
    </item>
    <summary>No summary available</summary>
</inventory>
```

you could reference the `description` element at the same level of the hierarchy using the relative path:

```
../description
```

You can select siblings of the current node by following these steps:

1. Type *../sibling*, where sibling is the name of node that's at the same level of the node tree as the current node, as in <xsl:value-of select="../item"/>.

2. Alternatively, specify a child node of a sibling by typing *../sibling/child*, such as <xsl:value-of select="../item/item_type"/>.

Referencing Child Nodes

You can access child nodes of the current context node by referencing the name of the child node. The following example matches all `item_type` elements that are child nodes of the current context node:

```
<xsl:value-of select="item_type"/>
```

Essentially, the direct name reference tells XPath to go to the next lower level in the node tree hierarchy. For example, if the current context is processing `item` elements based on this input document:

```
<?xml version="1.0" ?>
<inventory>
    <item tracking_number="459323" manufacturer="Not
listed">
        <item_type>Fiberglass Prehung Entry
Door</item_type>
        <description>6-panel left-hand inswing entry
door, primed, white</description>
    </item>
    <item tracking_number="459789" manufacturer="Not
listed">
        <item_type>Steel Prehung Entry
Door</item_type>
        <description>4-panel left-hand inswing entry
door, primed, black, steel</description>
    </item>
</inventory>
```

the elements selected by the value-of select="item_type" declaration are:

```
<item_type>Fiberglass Prehung Entry Door</item_type>
<item_type>Steel Prehung Entry Door</item_type>
```

You can use relative paths that reference more than one level in the hierarchy as well. To do this, you reference the immediate child nodes that you want to work with and then separate each subsequent level of nodes below this node with a slash (/). For example, if the node tree looked like this:

```
-inventory
   -item
      -item_type
         -code
         -label
```

```
              -manufacturer
          -description
       -item
          -item_type
             -code
             -label
             -manufacturer
          -description
       -summary
```

and the current context node is an `item` node, you could reference the code, `label`, and `manufacturer` sub nodes with the following relative paths:

```
item_type/code
item_type/label
item_type/manufacturer
```

You could use these relative paths in match or select attributes of XSLT elements, such as:

```
<xsl:template match="item">
     <tr>
       <td>
         <xsl:value-of select="item/code"/>
       </td>
       <td>
         <xsl:value-of select="item/label"/>
       </td>
       <td>
         <xsl:value-of
select="item/manufacturer"/>
       </td>
     </tr>
</xsl:template>
```

You can select children of the current node by following these steps:

1. Type ***child***, where child is the name of the node contained within the current context node.

2. Optionally, type **/grandchild** to specify a node set contained in the referenced child node. Repeat this step to go farther down the hierarchy.

The result should look similar to the following:

```
<xsl:value-of select="child/grandchild"/>
```

18. Using Absolute XPath Expressions

In addition to being able to reference nodes using relative paths, you can use absolute paths as well. An absolute location path always starts with a slash, which tells the XSLT processor to start with the root element regardless of the current context and then go on to specify the exact path to the node you want to work with. For example, if the node hierarchy for a document looked like this:

```
-inventory
   -item
      -item_type
         -code
         -label
         -manufacturer
      -description
   -item
      -item_type
         -code
         -label
         -manufacturer
      -description
   -summary
```

the corresponding absolute paths to nodes in the document are

- **/inventory/item** The absolute path to top-level item nodes
- **/inventory/item/item_type** The absolute path to item_type nodes that are child nodes of the top-level node item
- **/inventory/item/item_type/code** The absolute path to code nodes that are child nodes of the item_type node, which are in turn child nodes of the top-level node item
- **/inventory/item/item_type/label** The absolute path to label nodes that are child nodes of the item_type node, which are in turn child nodes of the top-level node item

- **/inventory/item/item_type/manufacturer** The absolute path to manufacturer nodes that are child nodes of the item_type node, which are in turn child nodes of the top-level node item
- **/inventory/item/description** The absolute path to description nodes that are child nodes of the top-level node item
- **/inventory/summary** The absolute path to top-level summary nodes

To disregard the current context and specify an absolute path to a node, follow these steps:

1. Type / to indicate that you're specifying an absolute path that starts at the root node.

2. Type *root*, where *root* is the name of the root node.

3. Type */container*, where *container* is the name of the element on the next level that contains the desired node. Repeat this step as necessary until you've specified all the ancestors of the node you're looking for.

4. Type */element*, where *element* is the name of the element that you want to select or match.

The result should look similar to the following:

```
<xsl:value-of select="/root/container/element"/>
```

19. Locating Other Nodes

XPath locations don't have to reference element nodes. They can also reference attribute, text, comment, and processing instruction nodes. Techniques for working with these node types are discussed in the following sections.

> **Note** Don't worry, you don't have to learn a whole new syntax to locate nonelement nodes. Everything you learned about locating elements applies to attribute, text, comment, and processing instruction nodes as well.

Working with Attribute Nodes

You reference attribute nodes using the at sign (@), followed by the name of the attribute. For example, if you wanted to reference an attribute called `tracking_number`, you'd use the XPath expression:

`@tracking_number`

As with elements, attributes can be located using relative or absolute paths. This means you could select the current context node's `tracking_number` attribute with the following declaration:

`<xsl:value-of select="@tracking_number"/>`

and that you could reference the relative path to another element's attribute, such as:

`<xsl:value-of select="item/@tracking_number"/>`

Here, you reference the tracking number attribute of the item element that's a child of the current context node.

Following the techniques discussed previously in this text, you could reference attributes of parent elements as well, such as:

```
<xsl:value-of select="../@tracking_number"/>
```

and attributes of sibling elements, such as:

```
<xsl:value-of select="../item/@tracking_number"/>
```

You could also reference the absolute path to another element's attribute, such as:

```
<xsl:value-of
select="/inventory/item/@tracking_number"/>
```

Regardless of the technique you use, the result is the same. The value of the attribute is output at the current location in the output document. For example, if the current context pointed to the `item` element that contained a `tracking_number` attribute and you wanted to display its value, you'd use the following template rule to do this:

```
<xsl:template match="item">
  <p>
    <xsl:value-of select="@tracking_number"/>
  </p>
</xsl:template>
```

Of course, a rule that processes an attribute doesn't have to be the only selection in a template. You could define multiple selections as well, such as:

```
<xsl:template match="item">
  <p>
    <xsl:value-of select="@tracking_number"/>,
    <xsl:value-of select="item_type"/>,
    <xsl:value-of select="description"/>
  </p>
</xsl:template>
```

or

```
<xsl:template match="item">
  <tr>
    <td>
      <xsl:value-of select="@tracking_number"/>
    </td>
```

```
    <td>
      <xsl:value-of select="item_type"/>
    </td>
    <td>
      <xsl:value-of select="description"/>
    </td>
  </tr>
</xsl:template>
```

You could also create a separate template rule for an attribute, such as:

```
<xsl:template match="/">
    <html>
      <body>
  <xsl:apply-templates
select="/inventory/item/item_type/@tracking_number"/
>
  <xsl:apply-templates
select="/inventory/item/description"/>
      </body>
    </html>
</xsl:template>

<xsl:template
match="/inventory/item/item_type/@tracking_number">
  <h1>
    <xsl:value-of select="."/>
  </h1>
</xsl:template>

<xsl:template match="/inventory/item/description">
  <p>
    <xsl:value-of select="."/>
  </p>
</xsl:template>
```

To select a node's attribute or attributes, follow these steps:

1. Specify the absolute or relative path to the attribute that you want to select or match. If the attribute is contained in the current context node, you don't need to do this.

2. Type **@attribute**, where *attribute* is the name of the attribute you want to work with. Or type **@*** to select all attributes of the current or specified element.

The result should look similar to the following:

```
<xsl:value-of select="element/@attribute"/>
```

Working with Text Nodes

If an element contains text or CDATA sections, you can use the text() node test to select and display that text. For example, if you wanted to select the text and then do something with it, you could define a template rule like this:

```
<xsl:template match="item">
  <xsl:apply-templates select="item_type/text()"/>
</xsl:template>

<xsl:template match="item_type/text()">
  <p>
    <xsl:value-of select="."/>
  </p>
</xsl:template>
```

Or you could display the text directly using a value-of declaration like this:

```
<xsl:template match="item">
  <p>
    <xsl:value-of select="item_type/text()"/>
  </p>
</xsl:template>
```

Keep in mind that the text() node test selects all the text-node children of the context node. This means that the result is always the concatenation of all text and CDATA sections that an element contains.

To display the text associated with an element, follow these steps:

1. Specify the absolute or relative path to the element that contains the text you want to select. If the text is contained in the current context node, you don't need to do this.

2. Type **text()**.

The result should look similar to the following:

```
<xsl:value-of select="element/text()"/>
```

Working with Comment Nodes

To access comment nodes, you use the comment() node test. Working with comment nodes is similar to working with text nodes. If you wanted to access the comment node associated with an item element, you could use a relative XPath expression, such as item/comment(), or an absolute XPath expression, such as /inventory/item/comment().

A template rule that works with a comment node could look like this:

```
<xsl:template match="item">
  <xsl:apply-templates
select="item_type/comment()"/>
</xsl:template>

<xsl:template match="item_type/comment()">
  <p>
    <xsl:value-of select="."/>
  </p>
</xsl:template>
```

Or you could display the comment text directly using a value-of declaration like this:

```
<xsl:template match="item">
  <p>
    <xsl:value-of select="item_type/comment()"/>
```

```
        </p>
    </xsl:template>
```

The comment() node test selects all the comment-node children of the context node. This means that the result is always the concatenation of all comments that an element contains.

To display the comment text associated with an element, follow these steps:

1. Specify the absolute or relative path to the element that contains the comment text you want to select. If the comment text is contained in the current context node, you don't need to do this.

2. Type comment().

The result should look similar to the following:

```
<xsl:value-of select="element/comment()"/>
```

Working with Processing Instruction Nodes

You use the processing-instruction() node test to access processing instruction nodes. As with other node types, you can access processing instruction nodes using relative or absolute XPath locations, such as ../processing-instruction() or /inventory/item/processing-instruction().

By default, this node test selects the text of all processing-instruction-node children of the context node. As a result, results returned by the processing-instruction() node test contain the concatenation of all processing instructions that an element contains. Because processing instructions have two parts: a name and a value, you can also reference specific processing instructions by name. The format you follow is:

```
processing-instruction('name')
```

where name is the actual name of the processing instruction. For example, if you wanted to access the `xml-stylesheet` processing instruction, you'd use the value:

```
processing-instruction('xml-stylesheet')
```

Here, the XSLT processor would select all processing-instruction-node children of the context node that have the name xml-stylesheet.

To display the contents of processing instructions associated with an element, follow these steps:

1. Specify the absolute or relative path to the element that contains the processing instruction you want to select. If the processing instruction is contained in the current context node, you don't need to do this.

2. With named processing instructions, you can type **processing-instruction(*'name'*)**, where name is the name of the processing instruction that you want to select. Or you can select all processing instructions associated with the current or specified element by typing **processing-instruction()**.

The result should look similar to the following:

```
<xsl:value-of select="element/processing-
instruction('name')"/>
```

20. Using Namespaces with Element and Attribute Nodes

XSLT processors track namespaces using namespace nodes. Every element and attribute node defined in a document can have a namespace associated with it. Whenever a namespace is defined, you must reference the qualified name in your XSLT stylesheets. As discussed in *XML, DTDs, Schemas: The Personal Trainer*, a qualified name has two parts:

- A namespace prefix
- A local part

and follows the form:

```
namespace_prefix:local_part
```

This means that the qualified name for an `item` element in the inv namespace is `inv:item` and this element would be used in a document like this:

```
<inv:item>
...
</inv:item>
```

XPath defines three functions that allow you to work with element and attribute names. These functions are

- **name()** Returns the qualified name of an element or attribute. For the inv:item element, the function would return inv:item.
- **local-name()** Returns the local-part name of an element or attribute. For the inv:item element, the function would return item.
- **namespace-uri()** Returns the namespace prefix associated with an element or attribute. For the inv:item element, the function would return inv.

You can use these functions much as you use other XPath functions. Here's an example that uses these functions as part of a selection:

```
<xsl:template match="inv:item">
  <p>Qualified Name:
    <xsl:value-of select="name()"/>
  </p>
  <p>Local-part Name:
    <xsl:value-of select="local-name()"/>
  </p>
  <p>Namespace prefix:
    <xsl:value-of select="namespace-uri()"/>
  </p>
</xsl:template>
```

To display a node's name, follow these steps:

1. Specify the absolute or relative path to the node you want to select. You don't need to do this if you want to work with the current node context.

2. To display the qualified name of the node, type **name()**. Otherwise, type **namespace-uri()** or **local-name()** to select the part of the qualified name that you want to work with.

The result should look similar to the following:

```
<xsl:value-of select="element/name()"/>
```

21. Using Wildcards and Predicates in XPath Expressions

So far the discussion has focused on the primary expression operators but hasn't discussed wildcard or predicate operators. The sections that follow look briefly at these XPath operators so you'll know how they work.

Selecting Any Node

XPath defines three operators that can help you select multiple nodes as part of an expression. These operators are

- * Selects any node of the principal node type. This means that if you're working with element nodes, you can use * to select or match any element node in the current context.
- **@*** Selects any attribute node in the current context.
- **node()** Selects all nodes in the current context regardless of type.

To understand how you could use these operators, consider the following node tree representation:

```
-inventory
    -item
        @code
        @label
        @manufacturer
        -description
        -summary
    -item
        @code
        @label
        @manufacturer
        -description
```

```
-summary
```

Here, `code`, `label`, and `manufacturer` are selected attributes of
`item` and `description` and `summary` are child elements of `item`. If
the `item` element is the current context node, you could create a
template that selects and displays the value of `description` and
`summary` child elements like this:

```
<xsl:template match="item">
  <p><xsl:value-of select="*"/></p>
</xsl:template>
```

If you wanted to select all attributes of item, you could change the
template to read:

```
<xsl:template match="item">
  <p><xsl:value-of select="@*"/></p>
</xsl:template>
```

Or you could select all child elements and attributes using:

```
<xsl:template match="item">
  <p><xsl:value-of select="*|@*"/></p>
</xsl:template>
```

Here, the | pipe symbol indicates a series where either the * or the
@* operator can be used in the selection. The result is that all child
elements and all attributes are selected.

Still, if you wanted, you could extend the selection node set even
further using node(), such as:

```
<xsl:template match="item">
  <p><xsl:value-of select="node()"/></p>
</xsl:template>
```

With the node() node test, all nodes in the current context are
selected, including element, attribute, comment, and processing-
instruction nodes. Of course, in an actual document you'd probably
want to format the output in a more meaningful way than with
simple paragraphs.

To select any node, follow these steps:

1. Specify the absolute or relative path to the nodes that you want to select or match. If the nodes are contained within the current context, you don't need to do this.

2. Specify the type of nodes to select or match:

- Type * to match nodes of the current type. Typically, this match is for element nodes.
- Type @* to select all attribute nodes of the current or specified element.
- Type **node()** to select all nodes of any type associated with the current or specified node.

The result should look similar to the following:

```
<xsl:value-of select="element/*"/>
```

Skipping Levels in the Hierarchy

The double slash operator (//) allows you to skip levels in the node tree hierarchy. This indicator tells the XSLT processor that zero or more elements may occur between the slashes and lets the XSLT processor search down the hierarchy for the node you're referencing.

To see how the double slash operator (//) works, consider the following node tree representation:

```
-inventory
   -item
      -item_type
         -description
            -code
            -label
            -manufacturer
         -summary
   -item
      -item_type
         -description
```

```
        -code
        -label
        -manufacturer
    -summary
```

Here the absolute paths to the lowest-level elements (`code`, `label`, and `manufacturer`) are

- /inventory/item/item_type/description/code
- /inventory/item/item_type/description/label
- /inventory/item/item_type/description/manufacturer

If you wanted to skip levels in the hierarchy using //, you could do this in several ways. Here are some examples:

- **//code** Starts from the root element and selects all code elements regardless of where they appear in the document
- **/inventory//code** Selects all code elements that are descendants of the inventory element
- **/inventory/item//code** Selects all code elements that are descendants of the top-level item element
- **//description/code** Selects all code elements that have the parent element description
- **.//code** Selects all code elements that are descendants of the current context node

> **Caution** Although being able to skip levels in the hierarchy is very powerful, watch out! Skipping through the hierarchy requires the XSLT processor to search through the node tree for successive matches, which can be very inefficient in large documents with lots of nodes.

To select skip levels in the hierarchy, follow these steps:

1. As necessary, specify the absolute or relative path to the nodes that you want to select or match. When you get to the levels that you want to skip, type //.

2. As necessary, type the path to the nodes that you want to work with.

3. Type the name of the element node you want to select or match. Alternatively, type @ followed by the name of the attribute node you want to select or match.

The result should look similar to the following:

```
<xsl:value-of select=".//element/@attribute"/>
```

Filtering To Match Nodes with Specific Values

You use the [] operator to specify a predicate. Predicate expressions are used to filter a group of nodes according to their position in a node set or according to a specific match value. XSLT processors evaluate predication expressions as Boolean values, which are either true or false. If a predicate expression is true, the node is a match and is selected. Otherwise, the node isn't selected.

Predicate expressions have the basic form:

```
path[predicate]
```

where *path* is the location path to the node that contains the desired subset of nodes you want to work with and *predicate* is the predicate expression that defines your filter for this set of nodes.

If you're referencing nodes in the current context, the predicate can be used without a path. In the following example the predicate expression returns all nodes that have a tracking_number attribute:

```
<xsl:apply-templates select="[@tracking_number]"/>
```

Numeric positions, functions, and attribute values can be referenced in predicate expressions as well. For example, the following predication expression selects the second item element in the current context:

```
<xsl:apply-templates select="item[2]"/>
```

If the input document contains at least two item elements, the node set for the second item is returned. Otherwise, an empty node set is returned.

22. More Options...

As with any sophisticated programming language, the XSL Transformations (XSLT) language defines structures that you can use to add branching and control logic to stylesheets. You use branching and control functions to conditionally process nodes based on the value of an expression. XSLT implements most of the classic branching and control functions, including

- **if-then** With if-then, you can specify what processing should occur if a value matches an expression. In XSLT, if-then structures are implemented using the `xsl:if` element.
- **if-then-else** With if-then-else, you can specify what processing should occur when a value matches an expression and when a value doesn't match an expression. In XSLT, if-then-else structures are implemented using the `xsl:choose` and `xsl:otherwise` elements.
- **switch-case** With switch-case, you can specify a set of values that should be matched and what should happen in the case of each match. You can also specify what happens when no match is found. In XSLT switch-case structures are implemented using the `xsl:choose` and `xsl:when` elements, and the case for no match is handled with the `xsl:otherwise` element.
- **for-each** With for-each, you can specify what processing should occur for each value in a set of values. In XSLT this concept allows you to process all nodes in a set of nodes iteratively and the element you use to do this is the `xsl:for-each` element.

In order to perform many advanced tasks, you'll need to be able to pass values into templates that are being processed or hold values temporarily during processing. As in a programming language, such as

Java, you use parameters and variables to perform these tasks in XSL Transformations (XSLT).

Parameters and variables can have either a local scope or a global scope. Unlike global parameters and variables, which can be referenced anywhere in an XSLT stylesheet once they're defined, local parameters and variables have a very specific scope and can only be used in a part of the stylesheet.

XSLT defines several elements that you can use to pass parameters to a template, including: `xsl:param` and `xsl:with-param`. You define parameters using `xsl:param`, and you pass parameter values to templates using `xsl:with-param`.

XSL Transformations (XSLT) and XML Path (XPath) define many functions for working with string values. You can use these functions to

- Convert numeric and Boolean values to strings
- Manage spaces within strings
- Sort and merge strings
- Extract substrings from strings
- Translate individual characters in strings

For example, you use the string() function to convert selected values to strings. You can also use the string() function to convert parameter and variable values to strings.

If you need to manage spaces within strings or the contents of a node, you'll find that `xsl:preserve-space` and `xsl:strip-space` are useful. `xsl:preserve-space` is a top-level element that specifies a list of elements for which whitespace should be preserved. `xsl:strip-space` is a top-level element that specifies a list of elements for which whitespace should be removed.

Thank you!

Thank you for purchasing *XML & XSL Fast Start*! This text was designed to help you get started with XML and XSL. Don't forget to review what you've learned and refer back to sections of the text as appropriate to help you with your further studies.

Lessons in Review

Exchange
Online

Your Quick Start Guide for Exchange Online, Office
365 and Windows Azure

Smart Brain
Training Solutions

Active
Directory

2nd Edition

Your Quick Start Guide for Active Directory.

Smart Brain
Training Solutions

www.ingramcontent.com/pod-product-compliance
Lightning Source LLC
Chambersburg PA
CBHW071212050326
40689CB00011B/2308